Praise for *Stand Your Ground*

"Debacles like Enron and WorldCom might not have occurred if senior leadership had followed Evan Offstein's premise of honorable leadership in *Stand Your Ground*. Indeed, leaders of all ranks in all settings can set themselves apart by following the principles outlined in his book. Drawing heavily on his West Point experiences and insights, the author points the way to the potential to transform not only the way we lead, but the way we live."

—Richard Thornburgh, Government Affairs Advisor, Kirkpatrick & Lockhart Nicholson Graham LLP, and former U.S. Attorney General and Governor of Pennsylvania

"In today's society ethics in leadership is a daily topic. *Stand Your Ground* consists of real-life examples of how ethics and honor in decision-making and communication have led to leadership success. I encourage anyone in a leadership position to read this book."

—Frank Beamer, Head Football Coach, Virginia Tech

"This book is plainly written and inspirational. It's full of new insights into leadership that come alive through analogies, anecdotes and metaphors—all useful to evaluating your own leadership. Making *Stand Your Ground* required reading at the nation's leading business schools would help eliminate Enrons from our future."

—Rick Stafford, Distinguished Service Professor of Public Policy, Heinz School, Carnegie Mellon University

"This book gives new meaning to the military axiom that successful leaders must hold the high ground; it convincingly shows both the 'how' and 'why' to the thesis that honor is the key to taking and holding the high ground in every leadership challenge."

—Jerrold Allen, Major General, USAF (Retired), and
Commandant, Virginia Tech Corps of Cadets

"The idea of quantifying honorable leadership is a powerful concept—especially for today's business leaders. Evan Offstein does not promote the usual quick fixes, but skillfully and intellectually describes the foundation and the building blocks of exceptional leadership."

—Robert J. Maricich, President and CEO, Century Furniture Industries

"Every university or college hopes its graduates will become leaders within their chosen fields and their communities and, possibly, beyond. However, leadership development is not often a systematic prescribed part of the curriculum. *Stand Your Ground* is a compelling case for how one of the nation's leading academies has embedded leadership development into its educational fiber. Evan Offstein has provided for our students and the rest of us a pragmatic description of the West Point formula. Here are the essential lessons for everyone who aspires to be a true, ethical, honorable leader."

—Robert M. Smith, President, Slippery Rock University

"A must-read for anyone searching for the missing element in leadership today. Evan Offstein accentuates the true essence of successful leadership for any era."

—Jeff Leischner, President and CEO, Thomas & Howard Company, Inc.

"*Stand Your Ground* is essential reading not only for every Cadet and their parents but for prospective new Cadets."

—John W. Gould, Owner, dlegal.com, and President,
Western Pennsylvania West Point Parents Club

"*Stand Your Ground* is an impressive and well-reasoned book that should be required reading for MBA students, managers, and leaders at all levels. Evan Offstein offers compelling contemporary stories and sound research to provoke every leader to ask the question, 'Am I an honorable leader?' His unique experiences as a Cadet at West Point, decorated Army officer, successful business leader, and now noted academic professor enable him to weave together a rich argument for the conduct of business in accordance with the time-honored traditions of America's premier leadership institution."

—Todd A. Uterstaedt, President and CEO, Baker & Daboll, LLC

Stand Your Ground

Building Honorable Leaders
the West Point Way

Evan H. Offstein

PRAEGER

Westport, Connecticut
London

Library of Congress Cataloging-in-Publication Data

Offstein, Evan H., 1971–
Stand your ground: building honorable leaders the West Point way / Evan H. Offstein.
   p. cm.
Includes bibliographical references and index.
ISBN 0–275–99143–1 (alk. paper)
1. Leadership. 2. Integrity. 3. United States Military Academy. I. Title.
HD57.7.O37 2006
658.4'092—dc22   2006015085

British Library Cataloguing in Publication Data is available.

Library of Congress Catalog Card Number: 2006015085
ISBN: 0–275–99143–1

First published in 2006

Praeger Publishers, 88 Post Road West, Westport, CT 06881
An imprint of Greenwood Publishing Group, Inc.
www.praeger.com

Printed in the United States of America

The paper used in this book complies with the
Permanent Paper Standard issued by the National
Information Standards Organization (Z39.48–1984).

10 9 8 7 6 5 4 3

For Laura, Madison, and Molly, and to
all those who aspire to higher ground

Contents

Acknowledgments

My debt for this book is owed to many. Unquestionably, the largest of all debts is due to the many honorable leaders that I spoke to and interviewed. Their thoughts became the text of this book. Since much of this book is predicated on honorable leadership at West Point, I am especially thankful to the cadets, staff, and faculty that took time out of their busy lives to educate me, and others, on the principles of honorable leadership. In particular, I would like to express gratitude to Brigadier General (Retired) Daniel Kaufman, the former academic dean. I will be forever amazed that he took the time to speak to me only four days prior to his retirement. With much going on at this special time, he thought enough of honor, character, and integrity to spend his last precious moments in the Army speaking to me about these issues. I'd also like to thank the Public Affairs Office at West Point and, in particular, the efforts of the always pleasant and hardworking Theresa Brinkerhoff. Two other honorable leaders deserve extra thanks because without them, I'm not sure this book would have happened. Dave Jones and Blair Tiger are not only tremendous Army officers, they are, without a doubt, tremendous human beings. Their ideas and contributions to this project are just too numerous to count.

To say that this book is "mine" is, quite simply, a misnomer. Sean Mikula, an honorable leader in his own right, provided many of the rich and colorful insights found within these pages. Furthermore, Sean was instrumental in the development and refinement of many of the core themes of this book and, because of that, has left his own "footprint" on this project that is too large to describe. Also, there is little doubt that without Sean's strong and focused feedback, this book would not have occurred, at the worst, or would be only a weak and poor representation of what it is now, at the very best.

As is described within these pages of the text, the scope of this project extends way beyond the walls of West Point. The sheer magnitude of this project required ample amounts of time, money, and effort. Because of that I must acknowledge the firm of American Strategies and the CEO of that firm, Brett Sciotto, for their financial and moral support that helped make this project a reality.

I'd also like to thank some special communities of people who either directly influenced the book or, in many cases, indirectly impacted the ideas found in this book through a rather direct influence on me. I begin with the Virginia Military Institute (VMI)—an institution whose existence is based on securing the high ground. In particular, I found Eric Hutchings and Gary Levenson to be leaders of character. In a short amount of time, these two individuals influenced my notion of leadership while working within VMI's commandant's office. Another organization that deserves special credit is Virginia Tech and the many people down there who continue to inspire me intellectually. While academics are often not thought as "leaders" *per se*, I found quite a few honorable leaders down there during my doctoral training. These include, but are not limited to, Devi Gnyawali, Terry Cobb, Donald Hatfield, Kevin Carlson, Jeffrey Arthur, Steve Childers, Bill Stringer, "Rock" Roszak, and Major General (Retired) Allen. The last community of people that I'd like to thank comes from Frostburg State University (FSU). While I recognize the financial support FSU provided to engage a project like this, I am even more grateful for the honorable leadership that I've borne personal witness to while here at FSU. These notable individuals include Ahmad Tootoonchi, Amit Shah, Danny Arnold, Tom Sigerstad, Tammy Shockey, Del Perdew, Nancy Rice, Connie Groer and Gloria Harrell-Cook. Tom Hawk, another colleague of mine at FSU, was an exceptional sounding board due to his experiences as a graduate of the U.S. Naval Academy and accompanying service in the U.S. Navy during Vietnam. No doubt his intellectual training at the Harvard Business School (MBA) and at the University of Pittsburgh (doctorate) helped him provide some theoretical and conceptual rigor to many of my thoughts contained within this book. So, again, Tom—thanks.

Several others, whether knowingly or not, helped in the writing, the reviewing, or logistics of this book project. It is an impossible feat to count the "countless" influences on this book, but I will attempt to do so now. My appreciation goes out to the likes of Ron Dufresne, Claudia Ferrante, Cynthia Cycyota, Brain Joy, Jay Morwick, Patrick Mifsud, Todd Uterstaedt, Russ Haynie, Al Moore, Robert Vedra, Mike Yankovich, John Mikula, Don Freeze, Jeff Leischner, Ted Williams, Jody Offstein, Pauli Overdorff, Allan Silverstein, Kevin Govern, Rick Stafford, Bob Maricich, Coach Frank Beamer, and John Gould.

Getting pen to paper is one thing, getting paper to press is quite another. And while it is not traditional practice to thank an editor from a publishing firm that is *not* representing the book, I feel I must make an exception. In particular, I recognize Connie Kallback who was the first person within the publishing industry that I came into contact with. I found her to one of the most helpful, caring, and responsive people I've ever come across. Like all projects this size, there is always a point where you feel like you're going to run out of steam or, worse, you can't see the end product. Connie provided hope and encouraged me to see the potential in this project, and by so doing, motivated me to see this project through to the very end.

When I think of my editorial team in getting this to actual press, the names Doug Savage and Nick Philipson are tops on that list. While I brought Doug in late on the project, his intellectual and writing abilities made an immediate and forceful impact to the book. I consider bringing Doug into this publishing equation as one of the very best decisions I made during the production of this manuscript. Kudos also goes to Nick Philipson, who has proven to be one of the very best in the industry. Nick's title may say something like "Senior Editor," but I think his informal titles are much more important. These include: friend, mentor, guide, and adviser.

Finally, families are so very important in so many ways that I cannot take their contribution to my own development or the development of this book for granted. I'd like to thank my parents, Alan and Patti Offstein, for instilling in me the principle of hard work, of which without, there would be no book. Also, to my wife and little girls, who provided smiles, laughs, and hugs during my quest to understand this phenomenon of honorable leadership. Thank you for making the writing of this book not a chore, but, rather, a fun-filled family journey!

Preface

Of all my life experiences, I think the writing of *Stand Your Ground* has been, by far, the most humbling. The reasons are far and many, but, one particular stands out in the forefront of my intellect. And it may be a common concern to many. The concern is best relayed through a series of questions. Think for a moment, as I did, upon the following—"Must one have been a professional player to become a professional coach?" or "Must one have had prior entrepreneurial experience to teach classes on entrepreneurship?" Or, more broadly, what level of involvement does one have to possess before they can become a subject matter expert?

This question was particularly troubling for me. You see, in the writing of this book, I was slowly becoming a subject matter expert in the field of honorable leadership while simultaneously coming to grips with my own limitations as a leader. In particular, one of the core themes in this book is that honorable leaders secure the high ground and, just after that, they stand their ground—they protect it. I realized that while I, myself, led honorably at places such as West Point, the U.S. Army, Corning, Target Corp., the Virginia Military Institute, Virginia Tech, and, now, at Frostburg State University, there have been times, quite frankly, that I missed the mark, meaning that I've not always led from the high ground. So while many authors write and become subject matter experts on a topic through their own authority and experiences, I do have pause here. Very plainly, while I'm on the right track to reach the high ground, when I look in the mirror, I still realize that I've got a ways to go. The journey, as it is for many, is ongoing.

There are many quick fixes, especially as they relate to leadership out there, full of all kinds of guarantees. I, too, now offer some guarantees—but not in the manner or kind that you'd expect. My first guarantee is that *Stand Your Ground* will deeply challenge some of your core assumptions about leadership, about ethics, and about honor. In many ways, this book is a contradiction to many of the things that we see occurring around us every day in our culture, in our society. I guarantee that you'll be impressed by a core demographic that we often overlook and, truly, underestimate. It is remarkably odd, and extremely humbling, to interview a young man or woman 15 years my younger and think afterwards—"I need to be so much more like them." While the world is caught up in the famous, the glitzy, and, often, the aging (or even dead) leaders, I found that, of all honorable leaders that I came across, the 19-, 20-, and 21-year-olds were the most intriguing. At a very young age, these young men and women possessed humor, flexibility, courage, responsibility, and, yes, honor. So I guarantee a rather uncomfortable proposition here. In *Stand Your Ground*, you'll learn less from people like General Lee, Lincoln, Churchill, or Mandella, and learn more from people like Sarah Dome, Robert Smith, or Amy Wiershem. For whatever reason, it is easier to learn from our elders. I found it takes high doses of humility to learn from those "junior" to us. But, if you can get through that, there is much they have to say about honorable leadership. I think we should listen more. In summary, *Stand Your Ground* is about changing the practice of leading, but, to get there, you must change the practice of thinking. I guarantee that if you do that, you'll be well on your way to the high ground.

Before turning a page, you probably want to know what this book is about. I'd say that it is about ethics. It is about decision-making. It is about communication. It is, for sure, about leadership. But, more than anything else, this book is about living. Because the book is about living above all else, the themes in this book apply to individuals, families, teams, groups, corporations, non-profit organizations, and, even, governments.

Even the best ideas, the best of theories need further refinement. *Stand Your Ground* is no different. For that, I'm counting on you, the reader. I would very much enjoy hearing from people about what they like, what they don't like, what seems to work, and what doesn't from *Stand Your Ground*. Don't hesitate to do just that! It may take awhile for you and me, but I'm sure I'll see you at some time or another up on the high ground.

Evan Offstein, Ph.D.
Frostburg, Maryland
www.honorableleaders.com
www.Stand-Your-Ground.net
email: eoffstein@frostburg.edu

Introduction: The Benchmark

The only safe ship in a storm is leadership.

—Faye Wattleton

Who's the best and how do we get that good? Answering these two questions is the premise behind benchmarking. Individuals, teams, and organizations all use benchmarking to improve, either knowingly or unknowingly. Whenever we compare ourselves to another, we are, in essence, benchmarking. Of course, the answer to the second question—how do we get that good?—can be answered best by first understanding how the benchmark got so good in the first place.

Benchmarking is used to improve manufacturing processes, quality levels, customer service, and, even, training. Few, if any, use benchmarking to improve leadership, but that is what I'm going to do here by examining the United States Military Academy at West Point—a true benchmark for great leadership. With the *who* answered, the purpose of this book is to focus on the second part of the opening question, the *how*. How do we go about getting that good?

THE POINT OF WEST POINT

The United States Military Academy at West Point was founded in 1802. Upon graduation, West Point cadets are commissioned as second lieutenants in the U.S. Army. Although West Point started primarily as an engineering institution, today it is much more. The West Point of today is a multi-faceted institution of higher learning emphasizing academic growth, military training, physical development, and moral–ethical enrichment for its roughly 4000 cadets, both men and women. These young men and women come from all 50 states and represent every race, religion, and creed.

A hallmark of leadership is the ability to consistently perform at high levels. At West Point, there is no such thing as "good enough." The notion of "satisfactory" simply does not exist there. Rather, West Point pushes and expects all of their men and women to achieve excellence.

How good is West Point you may ask? As of this printing, West Point ranks 4th on the list of total winners for Rhodes scholarships, 7th for Marshall scholarships, and 4th on the list for Hertz fellows. In terms of military, business, and political leadership, West Point has produced such notable graduates as Ulysses S. Grant, Robert E. Lee, Douglas MacArthur, Dwight D. Eisenhower, Alexander M. Haig, Brent Scowcroft, Norman Schwarzkopf, Pete Dawkins, Wes Clark, Mike Krzyzewski, Frank Borman, and Edwin E. "Buzz" Aldrin. Past presidents and CEOs of Holiday Inns of America, Eastern Airlines, Pan Am World Airways, Primerica, Pfizer, Coca-Cola, and IT&T are West Point graduates.

As a scholar of strategic human resources management, I've had the opportunity to discuss the leadership attributes of West Point graduates with recruiters and leaders from a variety of different fields to include the U.S. Army, the Central Intelligence Agency, the National Security Agency, IBM, Target, NVR homes, General Electric, and Corning to name just a few. Regardless of industry, sector, or organizational mission, the recruiters all tend to converge on a unifying theme as it relates to the men and women of West Point—their leadership sets them apart. Given a consistent track record of strong leadership, the prevailing expectation is that West Point graduates will succeed. Notice that this is not a question of *if*. Rather, it a declarative statement of *will*. To be sure, not all West Point graduates do succeed, but the way those few individuals are viewed speaks volumes regarding the level of expectation behind every West Point graduate. Those that do fail are seen as an anomaly, an outlier, a freak occurrence. The bottom line is that most West Point graduates succeed wherever they are, wherever they go, and whatever they do. Great leadership drives this success.

Organizations that achieve the recognition of "benchmark" all possess a defining characteristic. Without exception, these organizations tend to possess a fanatical passion about being the absolute best in one particular area. For instance, Lexus is passionate about quality. Michelin is passionate about safety. Apple and Sony are driven to be the world's best innovators. To stay in a Ritz-Carlton is to experience, first-hand, the incredible zeal for customer service and satisfaction. While these organizations are iconic representations of such principles as quality, innovation, or customer service, West Point is fanatical when it comes to the principle of honorable leadership. One thing became piercingly clear to me during my research in writing this book. No other institution in the world emphasizes leadership the way that West Point does. Can you identify any other organization whose institutional vision, its entire reason for its own existence, reads—"to be the Nation's premier leader development institution and a wellspring of values for both the Army and the Nation?" West Point then is the ideal laboratory for exploring the principles of leadership since they are so explicitly developed, taught, supported, and promoted as part of the fabric of West Point's culture.

This is not to say that West Point is perfect. No leader in the field ever is. Occasionally, GE has one too many defects. Now and then, Lexus may miss on customer service. Right now, there is some Wal-Mart somewhere that has an empty shelf. Organizations are comprised of individuals, processes, and systems—they are not infallible. And West Point is no different. West Point stumbled before and will stumble again. What separates the "benchmarks" from all others, however, is how they respond to lapses surrounding their passionate pursuit of their mission. From my repeated visits to West Point, I can tell you that no organization is as committed to preventing a future Abu Ghraib prison scandal. I can also say that no other organization takes it more personally when one of their graduates, like Al Dunlap, the prior CEO of Sunbeam, demonstrates poor and dishonorable leadership. There have been transgressions, but West Point has withstood them and has even learned from them, largely because of the strength of their institutional character and single-minded devotion to producing honorable leaders. "Benchmarks" always bounce back and West Point is no different.

One senior army officer whom I talked to, Kevin Govern, who was not a West Point graduate remarked to me about West Point's leadership development program, "Look at West Point to see what 'right' looks like." I took Kevin's advice and looked hard.

I approached West Point and the Department of the Army with two primary questions.

- How does West Point develop their leaders?
- Can other individuals and organizations apply these principles, tactics, and methods to their own situation, their own lives, in their own setting?

To answer these questions, I launched a comprehensive research strategy involving repeated visits to West Point. As a matter of fact, I made four visits to the academy with much of that time spent in residence. By my records, I logged just over 980 hours at West Point between 2004 and 2005. For those that enjoy *CSI* or just want to understand how I arrived at my conclusions, I've included a complete and comprehensive discussion of my research methodology in Appendix 1.

My number one conclusion from my research?

> *Any individual, team, or organization can significantly improve their capacity for strong and honorable leadership by consistently and conscientiously applying the West Point model.*

Central to a solid understanding of the findings from this research project is to appreciate the context, environment, and culture found at West Point. Briefly, I highlight and comment on some of the myths and realities that surround our nation's oldest military academy, West Point.

OLD YELLER

The days of hazing, yelling, and screaming are long gone here. West Point matured from a harshly punitive organization that relied on discipline and sanction to a developmental institution relying more on role modeling, mentoring, and coaching to build leaders.

I asked a senior leader about this institutional shift. Brigadier General Daniel Kaufman was the Dean of the Academic Board. He retired in early June 2005 after 30 years of service. He spent the greater half of his career moving West Point towards this developmental approach. General Kaufman granted me one of his last interviews just days before his retirement.

Regarding the issue of development versus punishment as a way to build leaders he remarked:

> We used to have an attrition model. We would set up 400 obstacles to gradua-tion and if you made it, you made it. If you didn't, you didn't. Now we have a development model. We really do want our youngsters to develop a self-concept of themselves as future officers. So what we tried to do is design experi-ences that we hope will lead to the right kinds of learning but then follow those experiences with some opportunities for reflection and growth. In other words, "what just happened to me" or "how do I feel about it." For example, at the end of Beast Barracks (intense freshman orientation), the first essay they write in English is "How has your view of yourself changed since you've arrived here?" And then those papers are given to the Department of Military Instruc-tion (DMI) and Plebe Military Science. So we've got DMI and the Department of English, remarkably enough, working in concert trying to get our youngsters to think about their own development asking "what's happened to me," "how's it changed me," "why is it important." So we're trying to build those sequential and developmental experiences over the course of 4 years.

He presses on about developmental opportunities,

> If the cadets fail to meet academic, military, or physical standards and they do have the kinds of characteristics that we're looking for, we'll give them the oppor-tunity to remediate. Take the course again, meet the standard, and then go on and be great. And so they're many more remedial opportunities now. In fact, our attrition rates have gone down 50 percent. Whereas we used to lose 30 percent of a class, we lose, depending on class, 12 to 18 percent of a class now.

Just because a practice is developmental doesn't make it easy.

A tendency of previous West Point graduates is to perceive that their grad-uating class had it the toughest of any class to make it through. Occasionally,

I would hear an old grad mumble, "The Corps has," which is short for the Corps has gone to hell. The intent behind such a statement is to imply that it is now too easy for cadets to graduate. I found these sentiments to be unfounded. The performance orientation at West Point is strong, pervasive, and unrelenting.

Most individuals and all organizations have goals. At its core, these goals involve the provision of a good or service. West Point's overarching goal is to win any and every war that involves the United States of America.

To win any military operation, the uniformed services and their leaders must perform at the very highest levels. There is little or no tolerance for failure. Probably for this main reason, the highest expectations and standards of performance are demanded of these young men and women every day in every way. One cadet described the experience at West Point as "hyper-competitive."

Further reinforcing this competitive atmosphere is the fact that most, if not all, of these cadets are hard-wired to succeed. One enthusiastic young lady who just received one of the academy's highest honors of being named an exchange cadet with the United States Naval Academy said to me with a wide-toothed grin, "I was the top dog in high school. Everyone here was the top dog in high school."

It is quite evident that these young men and women are hard-wired to compete, but the competitive atmosphere is further energized by the short- and long-term consequences associated with meeting and exceeding performance levels. Riding on performance is choice of branch, which one math professor identified as a critical motivating factor. To get military intelligence, aviation, or infantry, you must perform. You must be ranked high in your class. Future teaching and housing opportunities at West Point, not to mention graduate school, are also tied tightly to class rank.

You may be thinking what does an extra hour off mean? Who cares about getting an extra pass? Branch assignment or post location? These wouldn't drive me to perform you might say. Or this is just plain silly.

Remember that consequences, both in terms of rewards and punishment, are relative. A reward that motivates one, may fail to drive another. The idea behind this phenomenon is called relative deprivation.

The essence of relative deprivation is that the more a person is deprived of a given reward or privilege, the greater the motivational impact will be. The thought of a $10,000 bonus may motivate us to the highest levels of performance. Would that same $10,000 bonus provide the same motivational value to somebody like Warren Buffett or Jack Welch? Probably not.

There are few places that depict this phenomenon better than West Point. These young men and women own relatively little discretionary time and maintain few creature comforts. To get an extra pass or to wear civilian clothes off-post is the equivalent of a $10,000 bonus to these cadets. The point is that the little things, like 5 hours off, mean almost as much as the big things at West Point. If anything, relative deprivation tends to exaggerate the performance implications.

Earning my doctorate in business from Virginia Tech, I realized that in 999 out of 1000 cases highly competitive people thrown into an extreme performance culture is a recipe for individual and organizational ruin. By all accounts, extreme competition is expected to drive duplicitous individual behavior. The kind inspired by greed, guile, and self-interest. As a result, the team and the organization suffer. Politics and power games arise as people attempt to maneuver and politic for limited resources and limited rewards.

> *Can you be competitive without being cut-throat? Can you build a hyper-competitive team or organization without destroying it? Can you make cooperation and competition co-exist? This is our challenge.*

Despite this competitive pressure, the use of dishonorable behavior to get a leg up rarely occurs at West Point. And this is, perhaps, where West Point differs from most organizations. Cadets rarely lie, commonly don't cheat, and seldom steal. Instead of backbiting, in most cases, cadets enjoy and promote a rarely achieved cohesion and *esprit de corps*—all within a high-pressure, high-performance context.

I-ROBOT

One other possible myth is that West Point produces robots, not leaders. Again, I found this not to be the case. When the public sees men and women in uniform and similar haircuts, it assumes that they're all the same. We infer that because people look the same, they think and act the same. I'm not sure whether these views are widely held about West Point. If they are, they shouldn't be. I found that the cadets, staff, and faculty were not mindless drones programmed for only following orders. Rather, I found colorful characters full of diverse, creative, and, at times, contrarian perspectives. One such fellow is Colonel Dan Zupan.

Colonel Dan Zupan is a senior West Point professor of English. Not surprisingly, you get an interesting interaction when you cross a poet and a soldier. Colonel Zupan appeared to excel at both. An active writer, but also an alumni of one of the Army's elite divisions, the 82nd Airborne division, Zupan earned his bachelors degree from the University of Montana and graduate degrees from the University of New Mexico.

I asked him to respond to the following, "Do you think that West Point produces robots that can follow orders and execute, but not think?"

A pained and saddened look crossed his face. Clearly, I'd offended him. He offered the following response:

The problem that I had to worry about when I first got here is that we had a faculty member that knew all the answers so what he did is, he orated. There was no discourse. And this guy orated his particular view. He was not teaching philosophy and that was pretty disturbing. So, although we can talk about it, we are trying to teach the philosophical methodology so the cadets can learn to think about these things in systematic and rigorous ways and they're not going to get Dan Zupan's take on the absolute one-and-only moral system. That's so damned Un-American for one thing. We want to teach these young men and women *how* to think, not *what* to think!

A MAD, MAD WORLD

Necessity drives the push for critical thinking and decisive leadership.

I had the opportunity to speak to a remarkable young junior officer on an early trip to West Point. His name is Brian Wortinger. The 1995 West Point graduate and Darden MBA speaks in careful and measured sentences.

> We're putting these young men and women in very challenging situations, where you have young lieutenants and young sergeants out there, relatively unsupervised, in very stressful and dangerous situations, with very broad guidance on what they're supposed to be doing. So we absolutely rely on them to do what is right. Because what they do at the small tactical level has strategic implications. Now, more than ever, we need these people doing the right thing out there everyday.

These young men and women barely over the age of 21 find themselves in decentralized operations and faced with unstructured situations. On their shoulders is the responsibility of building new neighborhoods, reinforcing the local infrastructure, and preventing corruption and retaliation between warring people—all of which they must accomplish in a distinct and foreign culture. They often do this without close supervision, many miles removed from their higher headquarters. For these reasons, now, more than ever, West Point needs to produce capable and competent leaders.

THE MISSING LINK

Listen in to the first conversation I had with a senior editor from a major publishing house.

"I'd like to write a leadership book."

"Don't do it. Way too many of them. Market is saturated. You should've known that before even contacting me."

"Yeah, I know that there are a lot out there. But I don't think they're working too well."

"What?"

"They don't work. You know, not effective. And being the senior editor you should've known that before you answered my call."

"What are you talking about?"

"There seems to be an inverse relationship going on here. You know, a negative correlation."

"I don't understand."

"Every day, it seems that as more leadership books come out, we see worse leadership."

"Uhhhhh."

"Enron. Global Crossing, WorldCom. TYCO. Boeing. Martha Stewart. HealthSouth. Titan Corp. OfficeMax. AIG. Dick Grasso. NYSE. Citigroup. GE's InVision. The Penta...."

"Please stop."

"I can go on."

"No, please don't. I got it."

How low has leadership sunk? Albertson Inc., one of the largest grocers in the United States, is now locking up baby formula. In one case in North Carolina in 2005, seven individuals were arrested for conspiring to steal and resell more than $14 million in baby formula and over-the-counter drugs.[1]

How can this be happening with so many leadership books out there? Could it be that the leadership books and seminars are missing something? Could it be that the leadership pundits are emphasizing motivation rather than morals? Or communication rather than conscience? Influencing others instead of integrity?

Don't get me wrong. Communication is of critical importance. So is planning. Motivating. Strategic planning. Decision-making. Influencing. All are of absolute importance. But they all can get abused when these leadership skills do not rest on the bedrock of honor. Honor is the foundation of truly great leadership and honorable leadership is the West Point way, the only way.

True leadership cannot exist without honor coming first.

As I discuss later, it is difficult, make that impossible, to do the other things well if you fail to place honor before leadership. Motivational techniques will be transactional. Communication will be short and without rich meaning. Decision-making will be fundamentally flawed. The missing link in most leadership theory and practice is this very notion of honor. Honor must come first.

HONORABLE PURSUITS

Over the course of this two-year research project, certain themes or patterns emerged that help explain exactly just *how* honorable leaders become so good. These core concepts are particularly important for no other reason but to say that the greatest and the most effective leaders tend to practice these principles. Sadly, in almost every case of leadership failure, one or more of these principles were conspicuously absent.

Here, then, is an overview of the framework of concepts and a preview of what's to come in the rest of the book.

Secure the High Ground. A large part of this chapter is devoted to describing traditional approaches to leadership. Generally, leadership can be broken down into BEING, KNOWING, and DOING. Most leadership literature tends to focus on the KNOWING and DOING without first on BEING. At West Point, to lead right, one must start off by *being* right. Said differently, leadership begins with BE. Without the BE, it is impossible to lead from the high ground, which is the only place you'll find honorable leaders.

Antennae Up, Antennae On. The *moment* is the point in time in which you enter a decisional intersection. Here, your honor is either knowingly or unknowingly tested. The key, I learned, is to *know* that you are approaching this *moment*. Honorable leaders tend to be acutely aware of any and all situations in which their honor may be tested. To achieve this type of acute awareness requires that we erect and use an antenna.

Wash Away the Gray. Honorable leaders are often able to strip away the gray to see black and white issues for what they really are. As such, these honorable leaders usually confront and overcome the dooming forces of rationalization (the R-word) head-on and win where most people fail.

Be Big About Small Things. Being big about small things means that you care as much about the little as you do about the big. This is difficult to do since many tend to ignore or dismiss the small things as unimportant. This can't be farther from the truth for honorable leaders. To them, small things are incredibly important because they provide us an opportunity to practice for the big. Also, if we can't get the small things in leadership right, it becomes much more difficult to get the big things right. Finally, if one is not big about small things, the small things can snowball and easily spiral out of control.

Go All In! *Going All In!* is a passionate and deeply committed approach to leadership. Honorable leaders *Go All In!* by leading in both their professional and personal lives. Those on the high ground also *Go All In!* by telling the whole truth—never a half truth. Another important distinction here is that honorable leaders tend to *Go All In!* when it comes to means versus ends or process versus outcomes. To them, you must win, but, equally important, you must win by doing it the right way. In general, you will find that those on the higher elevations are 100 percent committed to leading honorably.

Who's Got Your Back? Honorable leadership is, first and foremost, a social process. Indeed, social relationships hold heavy influence over an individual's decision-making. Interestingly, honorable leaders travel in packs. They travel with other honorable leaders. In this chapter, I discuss the consequences of this social side of honorable leadership. We learn here that a strong BE begins with a strong WE.

Imagine That. This chapter focuses on the growth of honorable leaders. To grow, those that lead on the high ground harness the power of their imagination. In particular, I found that honorable leaders actively employ imaginative tools such as vicarious learning, mentoring, and role modeling, to become better leaders. Because of imagination, honorable leaders are able to view consequences of their decisions in terms of multiple time horizons (long versus short) and levels of impact or scope (large versus small).

Views From the Top. In *Views From the Top*, I illustrate how honorable leadership transforms an individual, team, group, and organization. Here, I depict and describe what an honorable person, relationship, and organization looks like. There is an undeniable correlation between honorable leadership and personal and organizational success. The reason behind this is quite simple. Honorable leadership affords competitive advantages that other leadership approaches cannot deliver. In this chapter, I conclude the book by highlighting what these competitive advantages are and, in the process, build a case for us all to pursue the high ground.

The whole purpose of benchmarking is really to learn from the best. There is no reason that the lessons learned here need to stay within the gray walls of West Point. I hope, and trust that you'll find that the principles outlined here can apply to almost any person, situation, relationship, or organization. If these principles are followed, we *will* get better. And that is a step closer to becoming the best.

1

Secure the High Ground

It's amazing how many cares disappear when you decide not to be something, but to be someone.

—Coco Chanel

WHERE IS YOUR SEAT OF HONOR?

Every year, toward the end of the semester, I conduct a small class exercise where I ask my students to reflect on their greatest achievements. I then ask about their greatest failures. One young man shared a story of his summer work at a new restaurant close to the Maryland shore. He had become the lead busboy and table hand at a seafood restaurant. The owner was a first-time entrepreneur and restaurant owner. Raising capital was a problem and the owner had to secure funding from a variety of sources including the local bank, credit cards, friends, and family.

My student went on to explain how during the month after the opening, the owner's three-year-old son had become sick with some type of disease. The owner had to take the son to Johns Hopkins for tests. Initial medical opinion converged on the diagnosis of leukemia. The owner had to leave the restaurant to be with his son.

While the owner was away, my student and other employees began to steal from the business. They would pocket cash payments, take beer from the fridge, one bag of frozen shrimp here, another there, a bag of coffee here, another there, and so on.

Because of the care that this young boy required, the owner missed many of the critical summer months at the restaurant. Although the cook was a relative of the owner, he was working too much on food preparation to catch the employee thieves.

From May through September, the owner missed most, if not all, of critical payments for gas and electricity, and to his food distributors. He paid his employees first—the very people stealing from him.

The owner's little boy got better, but the father lost the business. The restaurant closed and my student felt responsible.

Another one of my students was a student teacher at a local elementary school. She was receiving undergraduate credit for assisting a second-grade teacher on Monday, Wednesday, and Friday mornings.

Shortly after beginning her internship, she noticed that a little girl was coming to school upset, with red eyes. This happened frequently so she began to investigate. Out at the playground, my student noticed bruises on the upper arms of this little girl as she hung from the monkey bars. She suspected child abuse.

My student approached the second-grade teacher about her suspicion. To my student's surprise, the teacher told her to drop the issue.

"These issues are always messy. Always difficult to prove," remarked the teacher.

When my student pushed more, the teacher said that it was a small town and you don't want to get into small town matters. People know where everybody lives here. The teacher didn't want to start locking her doors.

To her credit, my student pressed on and went to see the school nurse. But she, too, was dismissive. And, to make matters worse, her supervising teacher found out.

"Put an end to this. If you don't, I'll put an end to your evaluation. You will fail your work study and you'll never find a job around here," she remembered the teacher saying.

But my student would not relent. She took the issue to the principal and demanded action. The principal responded. After some investigation, they found out that the little girl had been abused and that an older sister in the sixth grade at a different school had also been abused. The students were removed from their mother's custody and placed in a non-threatening environment.

The second-grade girl? Well, she started to come to class smiling.

I asked my student why she did it.

"I did it because it was the right thing to do. I was very scared. I had worked my way through college and was nearing the end. Teaching has been a lifelong dream of mine. But I thought to myself, "What kind of teacher do I really want to be? And, if I were in the girl's shoes, I'd pray every day for someone to save me. I've gotten good grades and I've done well here, but I'm most proud of this one incident. I didn't back down. I was strong. And the way I handled this event only made me stronger."

In different ways, these two stories help answer my critical research question. The crucial question of my entire research program at West Point and beyond is *not* "What do great leaders share in common?" Instead, the question that I attempt to answer is "What do the greatest leaders share in common that distinguishes them from everybody else?"

In the end, I found that the missing link between great, good, and horrible leadership at all levels and throughout all organizations was that of *honor.*

WHAT AN HONOR

This idea of honorable leadership emerged after almost a hundred interviews, a review of past and contemporary leadership books, and a careful review of several West Point documents relating to its leadership development program. In order to fully understand this concept of honorable leadership, I need to first revisit what I mean by the word "leadership."

One very hot Monday afternoon in June 2005, I had the good fortune of listening to Lieutenant Colonel Dave Jones, the Values Education officer for the Simon Center for the Professional Military Ethic at West Point. On this summer day, he gave a tremendous presentation to about 400 high school students from across the country, who arrived at West Point to see if it was for them.

During this presentation, he defined leadership as "providing purpose, direction, motivation, and application in order to accomplish the goal or improve the organization." After consulting several recent leadership books, I noticed a subtle difference between his definition and that of most others. His last three words "improve the organization" seemed to distinguish Dave Jones's concept of leadership from many of the common ones that exist today.

Toward the end of that particular week, I became aware of another distinction between honorable leadership approaches and all others. I noted that many leadership books attempt to zero in on acquiring new skills such as motivating, influencing, communicating, and negotiating. In a sense, this is seeking and gaining knowledge to develop a new skill set. Accordingly, we can refer to this simply as "knowing."

In many other texts, I noticed an emphasis on executing through planning, organizing, and directing. This is aptly called "doing." Although West Point and the honorable leaders that I interviewed there and in other organizations did focus on "knowing" and "doing," stronger emphasis was first placed on "being."

I found several leaders refer to this as the Be-Know-Do model, which is also clearly spelled out in the Army's capstone leadership document, Field Manual 1, *Leadership* (June 2005). The Be component of this model involves a person's attributes, his or her *honor.* More importantly, the Be directly affects the knowledge we seek and how we go about "doing" and executing. Without an honorable Be, the Knowing and Doing are rendered ineffective and, in some cases, can become downright dangerous.

Perhaps the most telling example of what can happen when we ignore the BE is also among the best known. By all accounts, former top Enron executives Jeffrey Skilling and Kenneth Lay were tremendously knowledgeable and intelligent men. Indeed, Skilling earned a Harvard MBA and Lay owned a Ph.D. in economics. Even the staunchest and most vocal of their critics acknowledged that these men were years ahead of everybody else when it came to the deregulation shift within the energy industry. In short, they possessed KNOW-how.

They were also skilled at DOING. Under their watch, Enron expanded through several acquisitions and buyouts. Before 1985, Enron did not exist. Fourteen years later, it was one of the top ten firms in total market capitalization.

Several years after the December 2001 collapse of Enron, beat reporters and academicians agreed that the story of Enron was really not a complex one. In fact, it boiled down to the BE. Lay, Skilling, and their CFO Andrew

Fastow, had the KNOW and DO, but lacked

> *Failure will always follow dishonor.*

the BE. As a result, the KNOW and DO were destined to fail. Whether it is my student's theft from the restaurant or the downfall of Enron, the great failures in life are because of the BE—not the KNOW or the DO. The corollary to this is that true success first begins with a BE focused on honor.

To further cement the importance of the honorable BE, examine the matrix below.

In Quadrant 1, you have leaders who really aren't leaders at all. They simply do not have the honor, knowledge, and capacity to execute. Under these conditions, the individual, team, group, or organization adds no real value one way or the other. In this quadrant, the human capital is harmless *and* worthless.

Move to Quadrant 3. Here you have leaders who have honor, but they never integrate it into their skill set, knowledge base, or execution plan. It is

Amount of KNOW and DO

	LOW	HIGH
HIGH	Quadrant 3	**THE HIGH GROUND**
LOW	Quadrant 1	Quadrant 2

Level of Honor—the BE

the equivalent to what some researchers would call "moral silence."[1] With moral silence, you may have morals but you decide to keep it to yourself. Here, leaders do not allow their BE—their HONOR—to impact their KNOW or DO. The value of honor is wasted.

Move over to Quadrant 2. In this case, you have somebody of tremendous knowledge and influence. There is also a BE, but not that of honor. Instead, the BE could be greed, selfishness, or hubris. It is under these circumstances that widespread corruption often results. Evidence could include the scandals at Enron, Adelphia cable, Arthur Anderson, or the New Orleans police department in the early to mid 1990s. This quadrant is characterized by strong motivators with high levels of influence. Without a doubt, there is a *sort* of leadership going on here. In fact, it would be the kind that Dave Jones describes, but without the last three critical words — "improve the organization." In cases like Enron, we saw tremendous "purpose," "direction," "motivation," and "application." But it wasn't for the good of the organization or its shareholders. Not surprisingly, this type of leadership is deadly and dangerous and is the antithesis of all honorable leadership.

> *To lead right, start by being right: Begin with BE.*

Quadrant 4 is what I call the High Ground.

Going Up?

Whether you travel from Manhattan, New England, or New Jersey, you must go *up* to get to the United States Military Academy at West Point, New York. The reason for this is simple: West Point sits on high ground.

Perhaps no other piece of high ground has meant so much to our nation's founding and survival than this particular area, 70 miles north of Manhattan. Indeed, West Point's role in our nation's history dates back to the Revolutionary War. Early on, both the British and American generals realized the strategic importance of the commanding plateau perched on the west bank of the Hudson River. In fact, George Washington identified West Point as the most important strategic position in the new America. General Washington transferred his headquarters to West Point in 1779. From this location, the American revolutionaries succeeded in stringing a 150-ton floating chain across the Hudson River. Popularly known as "General Washington's Watch Chain," it denied the use of this critical waterway to the British for the remainder of the war.[2]

West Point, and the war, was almost lost. Not to any specific battle, but to the opportunism of one Benedict Arnold. Assigned as the top colonial general at West Point, Arnold began bargaining with the British in May 1779. For a price of roughly 10,000 British pounds sterling and a commission in the British military, Arnold decided to give West Point to the English. Arnold dispatched a courier with the contract and assorted sensitive West Point documents to Sir Henry Clinton, a British commanding general. In what some now call luck and others call grace, the courier was captured and placed in American custody. American troops found the contract and plans in the courier's sock. The plan was foiled, and West Point remains the oldest, continuously occupied military post in America.

For these reasons, many view West Point as among the first American symbols of the power of honorable leadership because it was here that honor triumphed over deceit.

Toward the end of my two-year research campaign, I arrived at a simple, but profound, realization regarding the parallels behind the physical location of West Point and the almost one hundred successful leaders I interviewed: Throughout their personal and organizational lives, and not unlike West Point, the greatest leaders and the most successful organizations enjoyed tremendous benefits from using their honor to lead from the high ground.

Leading from the high ground is quite different from what I call low-elevation leadership. This high-ground leadership philosophy emphasizes honor in the BE portion of the BE-KNOW-DO leadership development model. By honor, I simply mean the attributes of leaders who shape their actions and decisions against a higher, usually noble principle.

This intersection between the high ground of honor and the physical location of West Point was revealed during a short interview with a U.S. Army colonel who was months away from retirement.

"It's our center of gravity," he began.

"What do you mean?"

Without hesitation he replied, "Well, begin by looking at our motto. Look at our monuments. At our crest, what does it say? It says, 'Duty, Honor, Country.' We cannot fulfill our duty to our country if we all act dishonorably. We are a beacon for others. We are under constant and continual scrutiny. We must conduct ourselves, even in the dirty business of war, with honor. If not, our duty is hollow and our country has no legitimacy. Yeah. Honor is what holds the ideals of duty and country together. Without honor we can just go ahead and bulldoze West Point off its perch and right into the Hudson River."

Rocky Mountain High

Honorable leaders are a study in duality. What to many would be contradictions, high-ground leaders are able to integrate into one holistic package. This skill appears to be a major source of their competitive advantage.

Perspective

To begin with, honorable leaders possess a mature and often wise perspective. Moreover, I noticed that this perspective often balanced short- and long-term consequences. Specifically, I found that many leaders understood that skimping or cheating on the short-term was bound to cause long-term problems.

In addition to this juggling of both short- and long-term perspectives, most of the honorable leaders encouraged, and, sometimes, demanded a diverse perspective. One statement from a battle-tested army colonel reflects this sentiment:

> With some junior leaders in the department I ask questions and sometimes I can see them trying to figure out just what I want to hear. I stop and lay it on the line for them and say, "I don't want to hear that. If I wanted to hear what I wanted to hear, I wouldn't have asked you." Be prepared, though. You personally have to be willing to take some pretty harsh criticism and some things you don't expect to hear, but that is how you make it better if you really want to make it better.

Thus, honorable leaders demand and deal with several important informational angles.

You don't have to be an expert hiker to understand that these feelings, these advantages, often arise as you reach the summit. Throughout history, the high ground has provided such perspectives.

Take a hike! No, not in that way, but take a hike to see what I mean here. On the high ground, you can see near and far. Also, you often enjoy panoramic, 360-degree diverse views from a perch. It should be no surprise that these sight advantages are awarded to those who stay on the high ground. In contrast, views from the valley or lower elevations tend to be shortsighted and limited to one direction.

In summary, honorable leadership from the high ground offers insight where others are blind.

Discretion and Freedom

Next time you go for a hike or climb, make a particular note of your feeling the instant you reach the summit. I've heard some people remark, "I'm on top of the world" or "I feel so free!"

Remarkably, I detected this precise sentiment from honorable leaders. This runs counter to the feelings of those on the low ground who feel that telling the truth or abiding by the highest standards of conduct are constraining forces.

One young lady suggested that when you compromise your honor, you, in effect, remove future degrees of freedom: "Whereas people would often extend to you the benefit of the doubt that disappears immediately if you show that you are dishonorable."

A West Point graduate who is president and CEO of one of the largest furniture stores in Pennsylvania told me about one of his furniture suppliers.

"We just stopped using that line. It was a loss to us, initially, because it was such a popular line of furniture. Our customers loved it."

"Why'd you stop then?"

"Because we just couldn't trust the main sales rep. He would lie or only tell half-truths. And, because of that, things didn't flow smoothly here and the customers who loved this line of furniture quickly despised its service reputation. Reputation is so very important here."

These passages suggest that honorable leadership builds your reputation and creates trust and, consequently, affords more freedom, never less. Conversely, lower-elevation leadership is bound to involve loss of trust and responsibility.

In real life, whether recreational hiking or in battlefield situations, more opportunities will always extend to those that hold the high ground. From the high ground, you can usually take a step in any direction you want—forward, backward, east, west, north, or south. The same cannot be said of those that are on the low ground.

Take for instance the Battle of Chalons. About 1300 years before our Revolutionary War, in modern day France, the Roman General Aetius used the high ground to defeat Atilla of the Huns. It was among the worst defeats for the powerful, and some say evil, Atilla. More important, it was the last major victory of Imperial Rome. It wasn't that the Romans had any special tool. Rather, it was just that Atilla had few options when stuck in the valley. In a sense, he was a sitting duck with only two real opportunities—advance through the line of fire to the high ground or retreat.

Thus, it is apparent that honorable leadership from the high ground expands, never restricts, a leader's discretion and freedom. Since leaders must solve problems and respond to challenges both inside and outside their organization, this managerial discretion is quite valuable.

True Sense of Safety and Security

The National Association of Securities Dealers (NASD) and the Securities and Exchange Commission (SEC) examined the brokerage houses of Jefferies Group, Inc., SG Cowen & Company, and Lazard Capital Markets for funding a lavish bachelor party for Thomas Bruderman, a onetime star trader for Fidelity Investments. The suspected motive for throwing a $100,000 party for this Fidelity trader was a simple one—these brokerage houses wanted a leg up in doing business with Fidelity Investments.[3] In addition to the firing of several top managers within and among these firms, regulators notified these brokerage houses in June 2004 that civil charges would be filed against certain traders.

Or consider the case of Shona Seifert. Ms. Seifert was a former senior advertising executive at WPP Group of Ogilvy & Mather. She was sentenced in 2005 to 18 months in prison and ordered to pay a $125,000 fine for participating in a scheme to defraud the U.S. government by artificially inflating costs on an anti-drug account.[4]

What these people, teams, or organizations miss that honorable leaders on the high ground possess is safety and a sense of security. Many of the low-ground leaders just mentioned must deal with the constant fear of investigation or sanction, both professionally and personally.

What this means is that honorable leaders don't need to devote much cognitive energy to the very basics of survival, safety, and security. Quite simply, when you act with honor, your behavior is above the fray and your actions are less scrutinized. In contrast, when you act dishonorably, you invite natural disasters in the form of more media attention, increased supervision, sanction, or the necessary constraints of complicated contracts.

The solid behavior and sound decisions of honorable leaders do not make them vulnerable to the same attacks and distractions that others face. With the fear of survival and safety removed, leadership energies can be spent on issues that directly translate into a competitive advantage.

It should be of no surprise that this parallel extends almost universally to the physical high ground that many desire. From the high ground, you are safe and secure from many of the common natural disasters such as floods, mudslides, hurricanes, or avalanches.

In conclusion, when individuals make the conscious choice of leading from the high ground they are, in essence, guaranteeing their safety and the safety of those they lead. Admittedly, this isn't as much competitive as it is protective. However, if you fail at protecting, you cannot act competitively.

Symbolic Motivation

This point can be best conveyed through humankind's experience with Mount Everest—the world's ultimate high ground.

Mount Everest rises over 29,000 feet above sea level. Modern attempts by Westerners to scale Mount Everest began in 1921. Two great adventurers, George Mallory and Andrew Irvine, lost their lives in a failed ascent in 1924.[5] Because of that incident, many began to doubt the ability of man to conquer this mountain.

Two men thought it could be beaten and refused to give up. In 1953, Edmund Hillary and Tenzing Norgay reached the summit, the high ground. From these two leaders, others followed despite the danger. Overall, more than 600 climbers from at least 20 different countries have reached this high ground. It began, though, with the will of two.

In investigations and inquiries, I repeatedly saw the power of indirect role modeling. Plainly speaking, when people see others reach the high ground, they say, "It can be done" or "I can do this." More important, other great people will tend to want to join you once you make it to the high ground. Because of that, the high ground will always be a special place with special people. The same cannot be said for those on the low ground.

Are You Up for It?

You may not make it to the high ground. There is no absolute, foolproof way to make it to the summit. Most leadership books propose quick fixes to serious and complex problems. Then we wonder why nothing is working.

High-ground leadership is just damned tough. Like those 600 people who have ascended Everest, few people really can or choose to exercise honorable leadership. In reality, the difficult ascent is what makes it such a special place and a place of the ultimate competitive advantage. A competitive advantage exists if you have something that others lack. Since reaching the high ground is such a difficult, time-consuming, and momentous task, you are, in effect, guaranteed a special advantage. Said differently, you will be in select company when you make it to the top because, frankly, few do. In the case of Everest, at least 100 people have died trying to make the ascent.

Climbing honorably also has its share of obstacles. Fatigue, apathy, rationalization, peer pressure, or the presence of a toxic culture can all work against the leader trying to reach the high ground.

Frank Borman is a great example of the difficulty of this journey. Frank Borman was a West Point graduate and one of the early astronauts. In 1968, he commanded the first flight to the Moon in *Apollo VIII*. He later became the CEO of Eastern Airlines. There he was charged with turning around the troubled airline company. When he arrived, he found a poisonous and toxic culture filled with excuses and blame. There was no sense of employee ownership and no strong leadership. Frank Borman tried to reach the high ground. He began by trying to repair an ailing and corrosive corporate culture. But, in an experience that brought a grown and honorable man to tears, he failed. He was fired by the board, and Eastern dissolved. Clearly, this man who flew to the Moon stumbled on his journey to the high ground. Nor did Eastern Airlines make it to the high ground—it literally died trying.[6]

It is important to understand that our own human nature and the will of competitors will constantly attack as you try to secure the high ground. For these reasons, be prepared to sacrifice.

Be Sure to Secure

It is not enough to *take* the high ground. *Occupying* it won't do it either. Instead, strive to *secure* the high ground.

Secure can mean two things. The first is to gain possession or to acquire. But you can't stop here. You must do more than just seize the high ground, which puts too much emphasis on the journey and the initial occupation. If you don't protect the summit by honorable leadership once you're there, you are destined to fall from your perch.

While we should all be proud of reaching the high ground, the real job begins once you're there and this has to do with the second meaning of secure—to guard from danger and risk of loss.

Initial possession is different from keeping. When Union forces, in July 1863, captured the high ground on Day One of the Gettysburg campaign, their task had just begun. On the third day, Pickett's and Pettigrew's divisions launched a violent attack on the Federals' Cemetery Ridge front. The

Union forces could've given up the high ground to Pickett's Charge. But their duty was to secure the land, to own it and hold it.

It is a sad fact, but many often let up once they reach the high ground and this is when the danger begins. Indeed, many of the executives involved in corporate scandals have not always been dishonorable or low elevation leaders. It would be difficult to fool that many people on their way to the top. Although I could not directly interview the Martha Stewarts of this world, I sense that many of these senior leaders let their guard down when they reached the top. Consequently, they exposed themselves to attacks and breaches. I know of one story where a young man reached the high ground and then used his honor to keep it.

This young man was Vietnamese and had come to America when he was 10 years old. While at West Point, he had a hard time passing English. In fact, he had failed it enough times to be turned back a year to a lower incoming class. During these failures, he had numerous opportunities to cheat or to plagiarize, but he chose otherwise.

As a turnback, he had to repeat English again. I talked to his mentor, an iron-willed lady named Laura Vetter. Her eyes were getting wet as she finished her story of this cadet as he was taking his make-or-break English exam.

> But he was not afraid; he was committed to facing the music. He said, "I'm going to do this. I need to do this. And I need to do this on my own." He knew that failing this time would be his separation [from West Point]. But this showed how much he grew within the past three years in terms of owning his own difficulties with English, taking total responsibility, total ownership for his failure or his success. He had the courage to let the chips fall where they may.

This young man passed, barely. However, that is not the point of this case. What is important is that he secured the high ground through his BE – his honor. We know that his honor and the high ground on which it rested were under constant siege. He could have cheated. But he chose to secure and to protect his integrity. Ask yourself, "What kind of leader do you think this young man will be?" Surely, one who can't write too well. I suspect, though, that he'll take others to the high ground. And once there, he'll be sure to keep it.

Reflect on the following questions:

- How much better would your team be, or your organization be, if you could implicitly trust each other?
- How much time would be saved by honorable behavior and trusting relationships?
- How much cognitive energy would be freed to explore other more important priorities if negative politicking were reduced?

- How much more competitive could I be, could we all be, by working in a culture of mutual trust?
- What's stopping you from moving toward this honorable standard?
- How can I get to the high ground?

Build Your Arsenal

Securing the high ground is no simple task. It is full of challenges. Therefore, you must be well equipped. With tomes of data and supporting evidence in hand, I believe I've found exactly the tools you'll need in your arsenal to meet this challenge.

Notice that I said tools, not weapons. The first tool is an antenna.

2

Antennae Up, Antennae On

There are two ways to slide easily through life: to believe everything or to doubt everything; both ways save us from thinking.
—Alfred Korzybski

IS YOUR ANTENNA UP AND ARE YOU SURE IT'S ON?

A couple of years back I left the Virginia Military Institute in Lexington, VA, to visit some faculty in the Washington, D.C. area. I left on the trip in my 1988 Acura Legend. By all accounts, this vehicle was indeed a legend. The driver's side door did not work; I had to enter through the passenger side. The sunroof leaked so I always carried a beach towel in the back. The air conditioner didn't work so I kept the two (out of a possible four) windows continuously down, especially in the summer. I always had to wear long pants when driving in the summertime since the leather and the padding had disappeared under my backside and upper legs, leaving only sun-baked steel for my cushion. Lastly, at around 190,000 miles, my antenna cracked and had fallen in front of my very eyes like a worn and diseased tree. Without this antenna, I was only able to catch one, maybe two, radio stations. So I sang out loud a lot when I drove my Legend. While I could live with most of the Legend's shortcomings, it was this lack of an antenna that would prove especially dangerous.

On this particular day, I had gotten up at around 4:00 A.M. to make it to D.C. by 9:00 that morning. I reasoned that 5 hours would be more than adequate for a 170-mile trip. When I had gotten onto U.S. Interstate 66 at about 5:30 A.M., I started to speed by signs urging drivers to "Turn to AM 560 for Beltway Traffic Updates." While the traffic seemed unusually busy at 5:30 A.M., the traffic was still moving at a brisk 70 mph. Besides, I thought, it didn't matter anyway because I had no antenna. I didn't think twice about the signs until about 7:30 A.M., as I attempted to merge onto the I-495 beltway. Racing at about 75 mph, with the eastern sun lighting up my windshield, I rode up a slight grade with no stopped traffic in sight. I was going way too fast as I reached the crest. On the immediate backside of this little grade was traffic—at a standstill. With a mix of instinct and luck, I pulled the steering wheel hard to the right and pulled off the shoulder of the road missing the car in front of me by about the thickness of my MasterCard. The Legend and I traveled about 40 feet until we came to a stop off the shoulder. The last of my hubcaps traveled another 30 feet. I was stunned and shocked. I had almost died because I was approaching a dangerous traffic condition, ignorant and totally unaware.

Five days later, I traded in the Legend and got a new car—one with an antenna. On repeat travels to northern Virginia, I always did listen to AM traffic updates.

What does all this talk of antennae, traffic intersections, and speed have to do with honorable leadership? Everything.

When I began this research project, I expected to find that the first step in the West Point leadership process would be role modeling. Of course, I did hear the mantra of "Lead by Example" more than once. I found, however, that the West Point approach toward honorable leadership actually begins with thinking. Put differently, good thinking precedes good leading.

I found that many honorable leaders, particularly the young men and women at West Point, were acutely aware of an approaching, dangerous intersection, or what I call "the moment." What this means is that their antennae are up and on.

The *moment* is the point in time in which you enter a decisional intersection. Here, your honor is either knowingly or unknowingly tested. The key, I learned, is to *know* that you are approaching this *moment*. While some people speed right through decisional intersections without much care or thought, this is hardly, if ever, the case with honorable leaders. Like careful drivers, many West Point young men and women demonstrated a sixth sense that recognized when they were entering *a moment* challenging their honor. Similar to what drivers would do as they approach a busy intersection, honorable leaders tend to be on guard and look for the yellow caution light. If there isn't one, they tend to string up their own. From there, they proceed with caution, awareness, and a heightened sensitivity.

I detected this mental preparation, and I believe this to be a pivotal distinction between honorable leaders and mere leaders. After all, it's when we're ignorant, unaware, and unprepared that real disaster strikes. The worst accidents are when you're blindsided with seatbelts off. A split second of preparation to tense muscles and cement your grip can make all the difference.

Let's look at another parallel.

When you research the great natural disasters of our time, it wasn't that they were any stronger or any more forceful than other storms. Usually, what separates mere storms from severe tragedies is advanced knowledge of the storm, which allows some freedom to prepare. Take, for instance, Hurricane Audrey. Audrey was a Category IV storm that slammed ashore just east of the Texas–Louisiana border in 1957. The storm killed 430 people in Cameron, LA, with its 105-mph winds. Now compare that with Hurricane Floyd in 1999. This storm with its 120+ mph winds plowed into the North Carolina shore right around Wilmington with a population eight times as big as the one Audrey hit. But, remarkably, only 56 deaths resulted. How can one explain how Floyd with stronger winds could hit an area eight times more populated than that hit by Audrey and result in almost 400 fewer deaths? The answer is simple— advanced knowledge and preparation.

I collected enough data points at West Point and beyond to surmise that honorable leaders tend to shun passive thinking in favor of critical judgment and acute aware-

> *Awareness allows you to prepare for your moment.*

ness. This assures them several advantages. Conspicuously, this critical and systematic approach to understanding and solving interpersonal and organizational problems allows honorable leaders to challenge and revisit assumptions that many take for granted.

Ernest Becker once remarked, "It is not so much that man is a herd animal, but that he is a horde animal led by a chief." The beauty of critical and active thinking is that it can reconcile both concerns mentioned here. Active thinkers are less likely to go with the herd. Becker's second point is an astute one—the danger in passive thinking is that you're easily influenced. This may not be a problem when the one doing the influencing is an honorable leader with good intentions, and equal consideration is given both to the means and the ends. Problems arise, however, when the one doing the influencing has dishonorable motives.

RACHAEL AND ROBERT

Consider the contrast between Robert Smith, a rising senior at West Point, and a young lady that I'll call Rachael. Rachael is the daughter of a close friend of my family. Her parents are well educated and what most would consider upper middle class. Rachael was a junior at Johns Hopkins when the incident occurred that I'm about to describe.

Rachael was home for Christmas break in 2003 and was babysitting during her time off to earn some money to take back to Baltimore. Right after Christmas, she was returning home from babysitting when she was pulled over by a local cop at a routine, alcohol checkpoint. The officer asked her for her license and registration. What she handed him was her registration and, by mistake, her fake ID that she used to get into bars in Baltimore. The officer arrested her and took Rachael down to the station. Admittedly, the officer was overzealous when he decided to contact the FBI under the guidance of the new Patriot Act. Rachel spent two days in jail and was released.

What is interesting about this story, however, is not the incident itself, but how Rachel and her parents chose to respond. Rachel's mother immediately called my father asking for the best attorney in Western Pennsylvania. The mother wrote to the newspapers, demanding that the officer resign or be fired. For Rachel's part, she was defiant and indignant throughout the process. Everybody she knew did this and she didn't see it as wrong.

I found a very different pattern when I interviewed the young men and women at West Point such as Robert Smith, a senior from Tennessee. I asked him about fake IDs and this is what he said:

> Yeah, I go back and a lot of my friends go out to the bars and I'm like all right, but I'm not going to drink and they're like "Don't you have a fake ID?" And I tell'em, "No." And they're like, "You really ought to get one." But, if you live by honesty, then you just wouldn't do that. You know, using a fake ID, while it may seem something not really big, it's the small things in life that really add up to make a person's character. If you brush off the small stuff and ignore it, what does that say about you? Is a $3.00 beer worth compromising my honor? No way.

This Robert versus Rachel case highlights the difference between erecting an antenna and driving an Acura Legend without one. Robert's antenna detected that the choice and pressure to use a fake ID was *a moment* and his honor would be tested. Conversely, Rachel never thought twice about the ramifications of using a fake ID. Keeping with my metaphor, she never put up her antenna. For that reason, she was both ignorant and unaware as she sped through her *moment*. Cadet Smith demonstrated both critical and courageous thinking. From a critical standpoint, he could appreciate the consequences of using his fake ID. To him, if he would compromise on such a small thing now, he might stumble when the stakes were higher. Moreover, Robert used courage and candor when addressing his friends back home to tell them that he wasn't going to do it, no matter what they said.

These cases also illustrate a key point that marks a significant departure from conventional leadership thought and practice. Whereas most ordinary leaders suggest that you need intent to have a breach of character, those who lead from the high ground strongly disagree. Instead, honorable leaders make no excuse for not knowing. To them, you can have a breach of character without intent. Borrowing from the field of law, their thinking is similar to the concept of negligence. At West Point, it is apparent that leaders see it as their duty to erect their antennae to gain better awareness. This is quite opposite from what we've observed over the last several years from those that lead in lower elevations. Ignorance and being uninformed has been pled as a defense to the corrupt behavior in the 1990s and 2000s of Ken Lay of Enron, Dennis Kozlowski and Mark Schwartz of TYCO, John Rigas of Adelpia, and Frank

Quattrone of Credit Suisse First Boston. How remarkable that men and women of equal or lesser intelligence and, in some cases, 40 years younger than those just mentioned, would never think of using such an excuse. What does this say about their leadership?

Without awareness, your honor is vulnerable to surprise attacks. In real combat, many of the challenges to the high ground occur at three specific times: at dusk, at night, and right before dawn. Research shows that at these times our bodies and minds want to relax. If you are a leader who enjoys a continual state of mental relaxation or blissful ignorance or even seeks blissful ignorance through such state-

> *Ignorance never protects your honor. Honorable leaders see a duty to erect and tune their antennae to stay informed.*

ments as "just get it done, I don't care how" or "I don't wanna know, just do it," then you are relinquishing your ability to lead from the high ground.

THE POWER OF ANTENNAE

Most electronic antennae are not unidirectional. Almost all antennae can transmit and receive signals from all directions. In a sense, it appears that West Point and other honorable organizations aspire to erect multidirectional antennae in the minds of their leaders. The mental antennae that honorable leaders erect can receive and transmit both short and distant signals. Let me give you an example.

Miles Nash is a 21-year-old African American from outside Pasedena, CA. He had applied to the nation's best schools, but won early acceptance to West Point and felt that he couldn't pass on the challenge.

He came in one morning to talk to me with an impeccable uniform with many stripes indicating that he's done well here. From the moment Miles walked in, I could sense that his antenna was up and engaged. This became apparent from his story.

Miles told me of a computer system gone awry. He was trying to do his math quiz online. After pressing Submit, he noticed that there was a glitch in the system and that he could've taken it as many times as he wanted and, in essence, would be guaranteed a perfect score. The teacher would've never known how many times he'd taken it. He had a golden opportunity to cheat. Instead, he and several of his classmates informed the instructor and only took the quiz once. He got a "C" on the quiz.

I realized that this incident could be explained by the mental antenna. Miles told me that he knew the intent of the system and that systems break down on occasions. He went on to say that just because systems are bound to break, that doesn't negate our responsibility to see that they're fixed. He went on to argue that a system's breakdown should never be our license to take advantage. To Miles, other stakeholders were involved who might get hurt. What if the system were down for me, but not for others? What kind of unfair advantage would I gain? How about the people who design or have some stake in the system? How can they improve a system if they aren't told immediately that it's broken?

Consider the case of US Airways. On April 16, 2005, US Airways experienced a glitch in their system. An online pricing error allowed several routes to go on sale for less than two dollars. Immediately, people jumped on this and the world community was alerted through web blogs, instant messages, and e-mail alerts. Never mind that US Airways and its thousands of employees were teetering on bankruptcy. To their credit, US Airways airline spokesman Chuck Allen said, "Obviously, if we sold any tickets at that rate, we'll honor them."[1]

Or consider the case of Orbitz when they offered the five-star London Lanesborough Hotel for $35 per night including airport transfer in a Mercedes and breakfast. The price was meant to be $350, but Orbitz honored the lowered price.[2]

These two cases illustrate leadership or personal development, both from the high and low grounds. Kudos to both Orbitz and US Airways for honoring their mistakes. They paid for their momentary incompetence. For US Airways, this must have been particularly difficult when they were struggling through bankruptcy protection.

When these two cases are placed in front of a person like Miles Nash, who stands on the high ground with the mental antenna up, the response is predictable. Instead of taking immediate advantage of a computer failure for personal gain, there is concern about the other stakeholders involved. There is an understanding of the mistake and an acknowledgement of true intent. I can imagine Miles Nash saying, "Wow, there's a mistake here. I know that a ticket should not be sold for two dollars. I need to alert US Airways that their system is down and that they're in trouble."

When talking with Miles, I realized that his antenna gave him views from many directions. Because of that, he built empathy for the diverse viewpoints and stakeholders involved. To him, it was really quite simple. He knew that he had made mistakes and that he would never want anybody to take advantage of him, so he didn't think twice about refusing to do it to others.

Does this make everybody who got a $2.00 trip from US Airways a poor leader? I don't think so. It just means that we can all hone our awareness and sensitivity to the environment around us.

When electronic antennae receive and transmit radio waves, they go around, beyond, or through different obstacles—including trees, air, or hillsides. I noticed a similar phenomenon with the mental antennae of honorable leaders. A West Point professor who had a mentoring relationship with a young man relayed a story that speaks to this point.

One of the more unique benefits of attending West Point is that you get in free to Yankee Stadium. Just show them your ID and you've got a free ticket to the bleachers to see a world-class franchise.

One weekend, a cadet had a friend visit him who was a die-hard Yankees fan. His buddy was not a West Point cadet and had little money. They wanted to sit together at the game. What was a long-standing joke became *a moment* for this cadet. His friend bore an uncanny resemblance to the cadet's West Point roommate. For a minute, he flirted with the idea of taking his roommate's West Point ID and giving it to his buddy so he could gain free entry to Yankee Stadium and that they could sit together to enjoy the game. But this young man realized that he was heading for *a moment*.

This professor went on to say how this young man looked beyond the Yankees and their quarter-billion dollar payroll and the face of the lovable George Steinbrenner to say, "You know, real people work there. There are parking attendants, concessionaires, and staff that depend on ticket sales for their livelihoods. Do I really want to go there?" And his answer was, "No." They never went.

And this is a key benefit to having a fully operational antenna. You're able to pierce or go around mental obstacles.

Indeed, real people do work at US Airways, at Orbitz, and for the New York Yankees. Honorable leaders use their antennae to see exactly that to pierce the corporate veil. Those on the low ground can't penetrate the superficial. They have a rough time seeing US Airways as anything other than a nameless and faceless organization. To them, Orbitz is a just a computer webpage. To them, the Yankees are nothing more than a bunch of overpaid prima donnas with a bombastic owner.

I found that honorable leaders tend to possess multidirectional antennae that allow them to see more, to hear more. Because of this, they gain greater empathy and understanding. To honorable leaders, the antenna is an essential tool. Without one, there's no hope of reaching higher ground.

Where Antennae Work Best

Looking back, I began to notice that, while the mental antenna itself was important, of almost equal importance was the placement of that antenna. Honorable leaders want their antennae in only one place—on the high ground.

If you reflect on that for a moment or think about the cell phone tower in your neighborhood, a simple, yet powerful, truth emerges. Mental antennae always work better from the high ground. Imagine being stuck in the woods with a hand-held radio.

> *Antennae always work better when they're placed and used on the high ground.*

Would you go to the valley to call for help? Of course not. You would move to the high ground. In reality, the best antennae are miles up in the sky with almost unlimited reach. These are satellites. But that same multimillion-dollar satellite wouldn't work if it were at the bottom of the Death Valley Basin. The effectiveness of all antennae depends on where they're placed.

From the honorable leaders I talked with both at West Point and elsewhere, I learned that the location of their mental antennae was instrumental in preserving their foundation of honor. When those mental antennae rest on the high ground, leaders tend to use and dispense information that is more transparent, more honest, more forthright, and more constructive. When information is received and transmitted in that manner, everybody within the range of that honorable leader's antenna is positively affected.

If you're unhappy with the information you're getting, don't check your antenna, check first the placement of that antenna. Similarly, when you look at the way you communicate with others, ask yourself:

- Am I honest?
- Are there always hidden meanings?
- Do people spend a lot of time trying to make sense of my messages?
- Am I *communicating* or am I politicking?

Your answers to these questions likely hinge on the placement of your antenna. Is it on the high ground?

To grasp the power of both the antenna and the placement of that antenna, look at one example.

I interviewed one young lady who was a rising West Point senior. The issue was "stacking" hotel rooms, which involves paying for one or two people then stuffing five or six in one room. This is what she had to say about hotel stacking:

> You didn't even really think about it before you came here, but now you notice. Actually, last year I was staying at the Army–Navy football game, and we were going to have four extra people staying. I don't think I would've done this before, but I went and told the hotel and they said, Don't worry about it; stay there; it's fine!

After a brief pause, she concluded, "You definitely become aware of things that you wouldn't have seen before."

This illustrates the power of the antenna. For this cadet, it gave her advance notice that she was approaching *a moment* and that she had better be aware. And since her antenna was on the high ground, she communicated to the hotel manager in an honest and direct way.

How refreshing is that? What type of immediate trust did she earn with the hotel management? Wouldn't you want this person working for you? Leading for you?

Cultivating Awareness of an Approaching Moment

If you were perceptive, you probably noted that this young cadet indicated that her antenna wasn't always there. To be clear, putting the antenna on the high ground is hard work—both figuratively and literally. Just ask the cell phone industry how hard it is to put a cell antenna up on the high ground in places like Seekonk, Rhode Island or McCandless, Pennsylvania. Zoning laws, public outcry, and stiff political resistance are preventing the erection of antennae all over this country.

I noticed similar resistance even at the United States Military Academy, but learned of techniques that honorable leaders use to help others place their own individual antenna on the high ground.

Find a Seeing Eye Dog

Through interviews, I discovered a special type of mentoring that appeared to exist at all levels of leadership, particularly at West Point. I call this the Seeing Eye dog phenomenon. It's a silly analogy, granted. But I'm using it to highlight a very important finding.

Specifically, I found that leaders help erect and tune another's antenna by calling attention to events that might otherwise go undetected. Lieutenant Colonel Kevin Govern, a senior West Point law professor, captured it best when he remarked:

> There are developments every day. You see an Enron scandal. You see Boeing.[3] You see what is going on at the Air Force Academy.[4] It is very easy if you make a little bit of effort to pick out every day something that deals with values or something that deals with honor.

In essence, Govern saw his role as that of a Seeing Eye dog. Without leaders like him, we're apt to dismiss, ignore, or just accept the events that occur all around us. People performing the Seeing Eye dog function force us to see and confront these public lapses of honor. It is easy to become numb to important events that occur all around us, or, to ignore them. These leaders help us see again. When they help us do that, our antennae are tuned.

Make Awareness a Priority

In preparation for the research and writing of this book, I canvassed over 140 leadership books published over the last 20 years for both academic and trade audiences. With very few exceptions, leadership practice and theory has largely ignored this topic of awareness. But "awareness" is where all leadership seems to begin at places like West Point and other honorable organizations. I found that higher elevation leaders and organizations never assume awareness. Instead, they actively cultivate it.

> If you haven't done so, find a Seeing Eye dog to help erect and tune your antenna.

The Values Education officer of West Point's Simon Center for the Professional Military Ethic, Dave Jones, made a clearer distinction between types of awareness. Anybody can be aware. The question is, to what set of stations do you choose to tune your antenna? Without question, at West Point antennae are first tuned to the "station" of honor.

Dave Jones told me that before every young man or woman enters West Point, a small package is sent to his or her home. In that package, a letter signed by the Cadet Honor Captain and the Cadet Respect Captain explains the importance of ethics, integrity, and respect for others at the academy. In addition, a CD-ROM details the honor and respect programs at West Point and every young man and woman receives a book on honor or leadership. The impact of this is profound. It sends a strong signal, easy for antennae to catch, that leadership at West Point begins with honor. In a sense, it tunes all antennae of those entering the academy to the reality that honor is taken very seriously—so don't be afraid, but be aware.

Making honor awareness a priority seems to work as confirmed by a conversation I had with one young lady, a student athlete on the West Point soccer team. She remarked, "They sent us the book *In Search of Ethics* before we even got here! And then when we did get here, that book became a topic of conversation. In the barracks. Everywhere."

ANTENNAE UP, ANTENNAE ON

Personal antennae are important in exercising honorable leadership and securing the high ground. You can erect your own mental antenna or the antennae of those you lead.

Some might argue that antennae are passive instruments. Honorable leaders would say, "Not so." Antennae provide us with vital information, which we may embrace or ignore. But, without having that information, we are doomed to speed ignorant and unaware through deadly intersections and *moments*. Ignorance is not a trait you'll see in others on the high ground. When your antenna is up and on, you're accumulating information that you can examine and process. Without this information, honorable decision-making and leadership cannot occur. Awareness is the first step and an important step in our quest to reach the high ground.

3

Wash Away the Gray

Nobody can acquire honor by doing what is wrong.
—Thomas Jefferson

CAN YOU STAY AWAY FROM GRAY?

Watch the last 15 minutes of the 1993 movie, *The Good Son*. In this final scene, a lady is holding one boy with each hand. She's secure on the high ground of some jagged cliff not far from Bar Harbor, Maine. The two boys are not so lucky; the boys are not secure. They dangle about 400 feet above the wave-beaten rocks and this woman's grip is the only thing keeping each boy alive. And then it gets complicated.

This woman is not strong enough to hold each boy in her hand. She realizes that to save anybody, she will need to release one of the boys to pull the other, using both hands, to safety. She is the aunt of one of the boys, played by Elijah Wood, who's been the force of good for the last 88 minutes of the movie. In her other hand is her son, played by Macaulay Culkin, who is the devil incarnate. Her son's angelic good looks have charmed most people into dismissing his cruel intentions. But the mother knows what her son is really like.

This mother is then faced with a mythic dilemma: Do I save my nephew, a good boy whom I see only at Christmas or Thanksgiving? Or do I save my only son who doesn't always act just right?

You'll have to rent the movie from Blockbuster to see which option she chose.

This movie clip depicts a "dilemma." A dilemma is a situation or a decision point that requires one to choose between options that are or seem equally unfavorable and mutually exclusive. In addition, most dilemmas have time constraints. The scene from *The Good Son* captures all three ingredients. One, both options were really unfavorable: either her son or her nephew was going to fall. Two, saving one meant that she couldn't save the other. Three, she had to make a decision quickly before her grip failed and both boys died. Given this definition, how many times in your life were you really confronted with a dilemma?

ONE IN A MILLION

Initially I thought that solving dilemmas would be a large component of honorable leadership and decision-making. After completing an interview with Colonel Ed Naessens, I began to revisit my assumption that *all* leaders faced dilemmas *all* the time.

Colonel Naessens is the director of the West Point nuclear engineering program. He received his doctorate in nuclear engineering from Rensselaer Polytechnic Institute. In his almost 30 years of army experience, he led and served on the ground in several conflicts, including Afghanistan.

His background is important to appreciate and understand his take on dilemmas. Receiving a doctorate in engineering requires one to look for many variables and alternative hypotheses in the course of research. The colonel's training suggests that there will always be another variable that might explain the research question a bit better. In short, his scientific research orientation demands some tolerance for ambiguity.

Colonel Naessens told me that of over one million decision-points, maybe only one would fit the definition of a true dilemma. His interview reflected a common belief that I saw at West Point and which honorable leaders validated in other settings: Leadership decision-points that are true dilemmas rarely exist.

Yet, to read media accounts and contemporary leadership or ethics books, you'd think dilemmas are all that existed. Most leadership books assume that 95 percent of all problems are complex dilemmas. In contrast, West Point assumes that only 5 percent or less of all leadership situations are true dilemmas. To discern which perspective was more accurate, I examined recent individual and organizational cases to assess whether they fell into the category of dilemmas or basic leadership problems with relatively "simple" answers.

Let's look at some recent evidence.

Employees who call in sick were at a 5-year high in 2005. Of all those people, 60 percent weren't sick at all according to a survey by the CCH, Inc., consultancy. Kronos, the major payroll and HR firm, surveyed 1316 workers and found that more than one-third of them lied about their need for sick days.[1] In another case, investment bankers at J.P. Morgan wanted to underwrite more Philadelphia municipal bonds. Toward that end, they got in touch with one of the mayor's top fund-raisers, Ronald A. White, and eventually paid Mr. White's law firm $50,000 for work it never did.[2] Then there's the case of Marsh & McLennan. This firm agreed to pay $850 million to settle charges that it rigged bids in its insurance brokerage business and that it directed business to insurers who paid Marsh & McLennan special "contingent commissions."[3] Or how about the case of James M. Zimmerman, the former CEO of Federated Department Stores, who was charged with perjury for lying under oath to conceal evidence of antitrust violations?[4]

In my random sampling of *Wall Street Journal*, *New York Times*, and *USA Today* articles, I could find no mention of dilemmas. In fact, most of the individual and organizational scandals boiled down to one observation—people knew the right or the legal behavior, but chose to act differently. These lapses of honor involve such activities as misstating earnings, destroying e-mails during an SEC investigation, using corporate/shareholder resources for personal benefit, lying to a grand jury, and selling stock with early or privileged information. My conclusion was that the West Point model is more potent for understanding and explaining current events.

About the time I was composing this chapter, a friend and West Point classmate called me with an issue he was facing at work. He was a senior quality control engineer at one of the world's largest specialty part distributors.

He became aware of a situation in which his company was not abiding by the terms of its contract. The contract called for one of their largest customers to receive a discount after purchasing a certain number of parts. For whatever reason, and maybe due to their lack of operational rigor, this customer did not realize that it had exceeded its purchasing quota to qualify for this discount. But my friend's firm knew. And they were staying quiet.

Saying that he had a dilemma, my friend called me. I just listened as my friend reasoned through this. At the end, he said, "Evan, sorry to waste your time. I think I wanted to make this a dilemma. But it's really not. It's really cut and dry. We signed a contract. We're in violation of that contract. And I'll make it right."

This story illustrates an important point—true dilemmas rarely exist. Rather, people mentally visualize the simple as complex. There is danger when simple problems are mentally magnified into dilemmas. Dilemmas insert gray into a *moment* that is actually black and white. Navigating a *moment* becomes more difficult when you see gray where no ambiguity really exists. Instead of exercising caution and seeing the intersection for what it really is, you can become confused. Imagining dilemmas where there are none won't get you through the *moment* and may leave the high ground vulnerable.

SHAMPOO OR CONDITIONER?

My field experiments lead me to the conclusion that much of the recent leadership scholarship assumes that almost all leadership issues are complex. Thus, we are conditioned to believe that many of the situations are complex when, in reality, they're not. Consequently, this mental conditioning prevents us from seeing the real problem. One possible explanation of this phenomenon is that sophisticated and complex situations make leadership seem sexier. It is as if we reason that we can't possibly be leading if we're only dealing with the simple and mundane.

Not only does this conditioning distort reality, it is inefficient. Think about it for a moment. Currently, we're spending 95 percent of our resources, including money and time, on dilemmas that we'll see only 5 percent of the time. By spending 95 percent of our training and leadership development on the complex dilemma, we have failed at the basics. By assuming that the simple leadership problem rarely arises and by spending no resources on it, we now run the risk of getting the simple wrong. Indeed, it is lying, cheating, and stealing that have caused so many to fall from the high ground. Recent breakdowns in honorable leadership involve simple transgressions, not complicated ones. More important, ask yourself, how can leaders ever expect to get the true dilemmas right when they can't even nail down the simple?

Although I found that West Point does train for the ambiguous gray that is the essence of every dilemma, they are particularly skilled at washing away the gray when it doesn't really exist.

To me, it brought back memories of the wash-away-gray commercials. Just apply this certain shampoo and the gray is gone.

Interestingly, this affirmative suspicion of gray, moral ambiguity stands in sharp contrast to the physical landscape of West Point. The buildings are the grayest of all granite. Some cadets joked to me that God had decided to make the winter gray to match the gray buildings and the academy's gray uniforms. Despite the gray surroundings, I found that honorable leaders there and elsewhere washed away the gray better than their counterparts.

With all this said, simple does not mean easy. Just because the answer is simple, the executing, delivering, or implementing of that answer may be anything but simple. Recall my friend, the senior quality engineer. He used his mental shampoo to wash away the gray; the answer to his problem was quite simple. However, he faced hardship and resistance when he communicated his concern to the plant superintendent. The first step, however, is to recognize simplicity when it does, indeed, exist.

THE R-WORD!

To understand how even good leaders mentally transform the simple into the complex, I undertook a systematic qualitative analysis of all interview text and related training documents. My results suggest that the best place to begin is to understand the *why* and then the *how* of this process.

Simple decision-points are rarely easy ones. In fact, I consistently found that the so-called simple decision-points that one faces in *the moment* have three defining characteristics. One, they require the leader to face reality, however unpleasant that may be. Two, making and implementing the decision is often unpopular with those around you. And three, some personal loss is associated with the decision.

Consider the case of Robert Smith. This is not the same Robert Smith whom we discussed earlier. This Robert Smith just finished his plebe year. He was skinny and tall. He called me "Sir" a hundred times during the interview and he was initially so formal in his respect for anybody his senior that the interview got off to a slow, mechanical start. Scared and a bit hesitant, he began to open and he shared the story of why he was here, during the summer, participating in this particular interview.

Rob knew about 6 weeks before the end of the semester that he was "at risk" for failing English. I asked him if he thought about cheating.

"Never crossed my mind. I could've cheated. It probably would've been pretty easy."

"How so?"

"Well, there are so many English classes, there are so many English teachers. All I had to do was get one of my buddies who had a different professor and say, 'Hey, can I look at your paper? Can I just borrow it for a second?'"

"Go on."

"We all have the same or very similar paper assignment. It would've been easy."

"So, you got an F. How's that a big deal?"

"Well, I tried on my own, failed, and am now at STAP (summer school) with no summer leave at all. I've been here a year now and I can't go and enjoy my summer like all my other friends here and from other schools back home. It's lonely."

"Then why didn't you cheat?"

"Again, I knew I was going down in advance. I could have planned to cheat. But if you do something once, it is easier to repeat the process."

This story is indicative of a *moment* with a simple intersection that is hard to navigate. In Rob's case, he had the courage to face the reality that he might fail English and, if he did, that he was at risk for separation from West Point. His decision was unpopular, especially with his friends back home in Mississippi who were looking forward to spending part of their summer with him. Finally, he faced personal loss. Because he failed English, his summer vacation vanished.

This story helps us understand and explain why people actually prefer the complex to the simple. Rooted in every move to make the simple decision-point a complex one is the motive of ease. It requires hard work and mental discipline to face the situation like this 19-year-old young man from Mississippi. The fact that making a decision-point or *moment* complex is actually easier than facing a simple *moment* may seem counterintuitive.

Remember that dilemmas are open to interpretation. There is no hard and fast rule when dealing with dilemmas. I found that leaders who are *not* on the high ground prefer to create these artificial dilemmas for that very reason. Artificial dilemmas allow you to avoid unpleasant realities. Also, they allow one to make a popular decision, not necessarily the right one.

And last, they allow a leader to make a decision that minimizes personal hardship. One particular slide during a presentation from the West Point Simon Center for the Professional Military Ethic caught my attention. It opens with the question, "Leadership, Character, and Values—what can make us stray from these?" The answer: "We take the easier wrong because we lack the courage to do the harder right."

With the "Why" out of the way, let's try to understand *how* leaders go about this transformation. By fully understanding this phenomenon, we are in a better position to set up safeguards and systems to prevent it.

Rationalization means finding justifications for things that we know are wrong. And it involves finding good excuses for things that we just know are wrong.

Early in my doctoral training for business at Virginia Tech, our doctoral seminars and research methods classes attempted to beat into our minds that there are no universal truths in research. A famous statement was, "A hypothesis can never be proven to be unequivocally true." For that reason, in research, hypotheses are typically supported or not supported; they are never labeled true or false. In the course of conducting this two-year research project, however, I feel that I've come to a powerful truth that applies in all situations and settings: Rationalization is the enemy of honorable leadership. As a leader, it is impossible to secure the high ground if you engage in rationalization. Think of it as quicksand. Once in it, it is difficult to get out. And it is impossible to advance.

> *Rationalization is public enemy Number One of honorable leadership.*

I've decided to refer to rationalization as merely the "R-word."

MAY THE FORCE *NOT* BE WITH YOU

Lucyna Turyk-Wawrynowicz is a high-profile maid who cleans celebrity homes for a living. More specifically, she cleans celebrities *out* for a living.[5]

In her first case in March of 2001, Turyk-Wawrynowicz used a client's credit card 16 times during a shopping spree at Barney's, a high-end clothing store. When confronted by the client, she allegedly remarked, "I didn't think you would notice." Just a year later and for a different client, she pilfered a $1000 suede jacket. Again she was confronted, but this time she got a bit more creative. Reportedly, she told the client that she would tell the media that she had been sexually harassed by the client's husband. Most recently, she stole $95,000 in earrings from Robert De Niro's wife, Grace Hightower.

Let's switch settings for a second.

Several years ago, I worked at a Target distribution center. While there, I had a Target teammate steal a DVD as it was going through the supply chain. He was caught dead-to-rights by security cameras placed around the 1-million square foot distribution facility.

I asked him why he did it.

"Target makes a billion dollars a year! Don't tell me they're going to miss one $12.00 DVD."

"Go on."

"Well, I wouldn't have to steal if Target would pay me more. I barely get $12.00 an hour. And what does the CEO make, that Ulrich guy, like $12 million! I'm just getting my fair share. It's really Target's fault that I'm stealing in the first place. Instead of giving millions away to the St. Jude Hospital, they should pay me more first. Target just doesn't care about its employees and that is why I took the DVD!"

I chose these two true stories because they share common themes that are reflected when somebody does the R-word. People embrace the victim mentality when they do the R-word. You can see this in the maid case. You know she's thinking, "I'm just a maid toiling away for these high profile celebrities who treat me terribly." It is more explicit in the case of my Target teammate. He argued that Target was actually forcing him to steal, a classic case of playing the victim.

The desire to shift the blame is closely tied to feeling that one is a victim. In the second scenario, the Target employee was searching for someone or something to blame. How about Target? How about the CEO? Or the supervisor? Nobody and no thing is safe from blame when someone starts the R-word. When leaders go down the R-path, they tend to see no connection between their actions and the results. For instance, the maid said that she didn't think the celebrity would notice. Similarly, my Target teammate minimized the impact of his theft by saying, "What is one DVD when Target makes a billion a year?"

Finally, we see that individuals attempt to depersonalize the real victim. It isn't Grace Hightower from whom Turyk-Wawrynowicz is stealing, it's a celebrity or Robert De Niro's wife. This theme is also reflected in the second case where my Target teammate doesn't appreciate that he is stealing from his coworkers, shareholders, or other stakeholders. Instead, he is stealing from a faceless and inhumane organization—Target.

One of Sir Walter Scott's most famous quotes is, "Oh, what a tangled web we weave, when first we practice to deceive." This quote is particularly relevant to the R-word phenomenon. Before we lie to others, we usually begin by lying to ourselves. Put differently, deception begins at home.

> Before we lie to others, we usually begin by lying to ourselves.

In the worst of R-word scenarios, conditions converge to produce the force of a "perfect storm." Here, individuals first deceive themselves to imagine that a simple leadership decision-point is complex. Then, the tempest gains momentum as they stack justifications for their excuses and faulty logic. The victim mentality, the depersonalization of someone or some organization, and the psychological distance between one's actions and their consequences contribute to this maelstrom. The moment leaders succumb to these forces, they have lost *the moment* and they have surrendered the high ground. When you examine honorable leaders at West Point and beyond, you invariably find a disciplined, rigorous, and almost fanatical desire to exterminate the R-word.

> *Combating the R-word is vital to honorable leadership.*

A RETURN TO THE SIMPLE LIFE

To this point, I've been descriptive, not prescriptive. We now know what the R-word is and that honorable leaders don't do it too often. Let's now move to the prescriptive.

Ironically, I found overwhelming evidence both at West Point and beyond that the best way to defeat the forces of contrived complexity is through purposeful simplicity. Nowhere is this more evident than in the West Point Honor Code.

The Backbone

The academy Honor Code is the backbone of the West Point character development program. Its beauty is the simplicity of its prose: "A cadet will not lie, cheat, steal, or tolerate those who do." At twelve words, it is the soul of every other development program at West Point, whether academic, physical, or leadership.

If West Point were alive, its spine would be Honor.

All West Point systems radiate from this foundation of honor. Without it, physical, intellectual, and leadership development could not occur. The Honor Code is the absolute minimum standard for all academy decisions, all behavior. It is the crawl stage of leadership development. Before honorable leaders can deal with more complex issues and challenges, they must first demonstrate that they can crawl, which in this case is living by the Honor Code.

At the very beginning of this research project, I spoke with a young man, James Kehoe. James is now an army officer, but when I spoke to him he was two months into his cadet job of Cadet Honor Captain. I asked him about the simplicity of the Honor Code. He quickly reminded me that the West Point Honor Code is a stepping stone to more advanced development. Cadet Kehoe explained how crawling leads to walking and, eventually, running.

> We have something also that we like to teach, and that we've been hitting on a lot more is the "Spirit of the Code." Instead of a "cadet will not lie," we stress that "a cadet will be truthful." Instead of "a cadet will not cheat," we stress that "a cadet will always be fair." It takes each part and it says, "Okay, not only

should you do the minimum, but you should go above and beyond that. You should be responsible and respectful." And that is the spirit of the code, and we try to teach that never should we go for the minimum. We don't do that in anything else. We don't just try and pass our classes with a "D." You don't just try and get your 180 [the minimum passing grade] on the physical fitness test, so why would you do that when it comes to honor? If West Point means going for excellence in everything, that's what you should be doing in honor too.

My discussions with James Kehoe reflect a consistent theme found in other discussions with honorable leaders: Once the simple is mastered, you can aspire higher. Of course, higher aspirations could be the high ground. That is certainly true at West Point. The "Spirit of the Code" cannot exist on its own. Rather, it builds on those twelve simple and foundational words.

As part of my research, I collected other codes developed by other organizations, some academic, some for profit, and some nonprofit. I compared them for similarities and differences. In

> *Build atop the simple to aspire higher.*

almost every case, two themes emerged. First, integrity guidelines or ethics codes as they are often called, were difficult to find. They weren't front and center, but were buried deep in a website index or in an employee handbook. In cases like this, what is not said or where an ethics code is put speaks volumes. Codes of ethics hidden deep in some hyperlink on a webpage are not easily accessible. For that reason, their impact is bound to be limited. Second, when I did find a statement of ethics or a code of integrity, invariably there were many words, usually in several paragraphs. Our thoughts, decisions, and behavior are influenced more by twelve simple words that are hard to forget than by twelve long paragraphs that are hard to remember.

AGREE TO ONE, TWO, AND THREE

Gary Klein is an internationally acclaimed researcher in the field of individual and team decision-making. Of particular interest to Gary Klein is how leaders make decisions under stress or, worse, in emergency situations. To that end, Klein has rigorously studied such professions as airline pilots, firefighters, and emergency medical responders.[6]

At the beginning of one of Klein's books, *Sources of Power: How People Make Decisions,* he details the case of the torn artery. In this little vignette, he details how a man was doing some home repair when he fell from his ladder. When he slipped, his arm went through a pane of glass. When the medical responders arrived, the man had already lost two units of blood. If he lost two more, he would die.

I consulted this particular book during my research because I found it germane to honorable leadership. Since emergency medical responders, firefighters, and, occasionally, airline pilots tend to deal with ambiguous and complex situations under severe time constraints, I thought their approaches could help us deal with the R-word and contrived dilemmas, which tend to manufacture complexity where none should exist. Like before, I found that one particularly powerful way to sift through ambiguity and complexity was a return to simplicity.

This is where "decision heuristics" come into play. A heuristic is nothing more than a commonsense set of rules that we use to increase our probability of solving some type of problem. For the heuristic to be effective, it must be short, simple, easy to remember, and easy to use.

In the case of the emergency medical responder, he relied on his training and, in particular, his mental heuristic to guide him through this life-threatening crisis. First, he diagnosed the problem in seconds, while the victim's wife screamed and cried. Next, he decided how to treat this serious wound. Realizing that delay was fatal, he directed his strongest crewman to do the stretcher work. Only 10 minutes elapsed between the initial alarm and delivery of the man to the hospital.

I found a very similar reliance on simple mental heuristics at West Point. Very early on, West Point mentally equips young men and women with what they call the "Three Rules of Thumb." These Three Rules of Thumb are really questions to be used when these future leaders approach *a moment* where their honor is being tested. The three rules read:

> **Rule One:** Does this action attempt to deceive anyone or allow anyone to be deceived?
>
> **Rule Two:** Does this action gain or allow the gain of privilege or advantage to which I or someone else would not otherwise be entitled?
>
> **Rule Three:** Would I be satisfied by the outcome if I were on the receiving end of this action?

Go ahead and take them for a test drive. I did. If just one rule is violated, you know that you're in danger of not surviving *the moment* with your honor intact.

I returned to my random sampling of cases and stories from the *Wall Street Journal, New York Times, and USA Today.* In each case, the Three Rules of Thumb would have prevented the fall from the high ground.

Consider the 2004 case of Frank Quattrone, a former high-flying investment banker with Credit Suisse First Boston. Quattrone was found guilty of ordering employees to destroy evidence during an investigation of share allocation in an initial public stock offering.[7] If he had taken 15 seconds to apply the Three Rules of Thumb, he could've avoided failure.

Or how about the senior managers at American International Group (AIG)? In one of AIG's earliest missteps in 2003–2004, AIG paid $136 million to settle allegations that they helped Brightpoint and PNC manipulate earnings.[8] Would the Three Rules of Thumb have worked here? It appears so.

Consider the rising phenomenon of click fraud. A competitor clicks heavily on a rival's Internet banner on such websites as Google or Yahoo with no intention of doing business. The sole intent is to artificially inflate advertising costs that the business has to pay Google or Yahoo based on "hits."[9] It is a covert way to sabotage your rivals by increasing their advertising expenses. Do the Three Rules apply here? You bet.

Armed with these Three Rules, ask yourself if there is a single *moment* that you cannot safely get through? I challenge you to find a single challenge to your honor where the Three Rules of Thumb would not help. They are easy to use and easy to remember. They provide clarity and mental acuity as one approaches a *moment*. More important, they illuminate the usual simplicity of a situation that might otherwise be imagined as complex.

The Three Rules of Thumb may not work in true dilemmas heavy with real ethical ambiguities. But that shouldn't matter much since true dilemmas occur about as often as Haley's Comet. It is important to note that a sequential defense is vital against assaults on your honor. Awareness must precede the use of the Three Rules of Thumb. If you aren't aware as you approach a

> *Enhance your honorable decision-making by relying upon the Three Rules of Thumb.*

moment, you won't resort in time to your three rules. So, awareness must come first.

NO EXCUSE!

It was Martin Luther King weekend in 1994 and I was at my fiancé's house in New Jersey. On this particular weekend, West Point must've been feeling generous because they offered a reprieve from Monday classes. So I had a three-day weekend. On the Monday that I had to return, we woke up to a New Jersey winter wonderland. At midnight, it began to snow. At about 2:00 A.M., it started to sleet. The ice changed back to snow before we got up. At 8:30 A.M., Mother Nature got really angry and changed everything back to ice. We called West Point and asked if we could take another day off due to the weather. We knew, of course, what the answer would be. No.

So at 9:30 A.M., my future wife, another West Point guy named Rob Salome, and I crawled into, you bet, the 1988 Acura Legend to make what is normally a 3-hour drive to return to West Point. On this particular day, the New Jersey turnpike became the world's largest ice rink. What normally took us 3 hours to do, took us 10. In fact, the Acura Legend was the last vehicle allowed on the Palisades Parkway before it was shut down to all traffic due to dangerous conditions. It was eerie. What was normally a busy and congested highway artery was nothing more than a glorified sled path.

Deer, otters, and I swear, the Budweiser Clydesdale horses, all passed us. We had to sign in by 1900 hours, which is the equivalent of 7:00 P.M. Well, we signed in at 7:10 P.M.

My tactical officer approached us, "Why are you late?"

I responded in total disbelief, "Sir, we called and did you see it out there? The only way we could've gotten here faster was a snowmobile! Is that what you wanted us to do? Come on, Sir, we risked our lives to get back here!"

"Wrong answer."

"Excuse me, Sir."

"No, you're not excused," he shot back.

"I'm sorry, Sir. I just don't understand. Cooped up in that Acura Legend for 10 hours must've made me dizzy. Cause I don't understand what you just said."

"Let me make it clear for you, Evan." He paused. "There is no excuse for you. You should have been here before 1900 hours. You could've left last night. You should've checked the weather. It's not my fault that you're late. It's not even Mother Nature's fault you're late. It is *your* fault you're late."

"You're saying that I can't even blame my lateness on a natural disaster, Sir?"

"Nope. And you won't be going on any more weekend escapades anytime soon."

To more fully grasp the potency of this concept of No Excuse, let's examine another case.

What felt like a lifetime later, I sat down with a plebe—West Point's version of a freshman. I asked him how often he saw people do the R-word.

"Doesn't happen here. Won't happen here."

"Why?" I asked.

"Well...this is the land of no-excuse, even if you do have a legitimate excuse."

I pressed, "Can you be more specific?"

"Well," I saw him hesitate. He was a bit nervous. But he went on, "Well, Okay. I'm a little embarrassed by this story but you can use it."

"Thank you."

He blurted, "I was asked to state the phonetic alphabet backwards!" Then he stopped.

The phonetic alphabet is common in the military. It starts Alpha, Bravo, Charlie, Delta and ends X-ray, Yankee, and Zulu.

"I'm not following here," I said to the plebe.

He continued with a small smile on his face, "Our minds don't work like that. Can you do the regular alphabet backwards quickly?" he asked me.

I thought about it for a moment and I realized he was right.

"Right. We're not programmed to say the alphabet backwards, let alone the phonetic alphabet. I tried to explain that to my squad leader, but he wouldn't have any of it. He reminded me that I had a choice of four answers."

I knew the answer, but asked anyway, "What are the four answers?"

"Well, they're not exactly answers. They're more like responses. They're 'Yes, Sir or Ma'am,' 'No, Sir or Ma'am,' 'No excuse, Sir or Ma'am,' and 'Sir or Ma'am, I do not understand.'"

"Which did you choose?"

His smile broke out to a grin, "I had to say No Excuse! I had to say No Excuse for my own incompetence!"

"How is this important?"

"I know it kind of sounds funny. It's basic and it's simple. But don't be fooled. This is important stuff."

"How so?" I asked.

"You can't make up excuses as you're going along. If you have the chance to make an excuse, it's likely you will proceed in doing whatever you want to do include lying, cheating, or stealing."

The importance of this No-Excuse approach to honorable leadership dawned on me as I sat down with Laura Vetter, an instructor at the West Point Center for Enhanced Performance. Maybe because she was a new instructor coming from Kansas State University, or maybe because she was trained as an anthropologist, but, for whatever reason, Laura Vetter nailed the point home for me.

"Well, first and foremost, I don't believe that there is a great opportunity for rationalization here at West Point. In fact, it's really a misnomer here. This idea of 'No Excuse' is taught to every young leader who enters through those sally ports."

She reflected and pressed her palms together. "Don't you see that leaders are responsible for everyone else. If you engage in rationalization, there will be hundred more rationalizations made. Somebody has to take the lead. Somebody has to be responsible. To be accountable."

Her soliloquy brings me to a significant point. It is tough to rely on excuses and lame justifications when you're taught early that there is No Excuse. Very simply, this No Excuse mentality short-circuits the R-word process. With No Excuse, you also get No R-Word. Laura Vetter captures a deeper point, though. Rather than spending time and resources looking for excuses and justifica-

> *The R-word cannot survive a No-Excuse approach to leadership.*

tions, honorable leaders search out and find responsibility and accountability. This stands in marked contrast to recent scandals where well-educated and senior managers, not 18- or 19-year-old men and women, have distanced themselves from responsibility or accountability.

It is necessary to call attention to this difference, without climbing on the high horse. We don't want that. We want the high ground, not the high horse. But, the very litigious nature of our society almost programs us to shirk responsibility. There are attorneys out there who make quite a good living promising us that we're not responsible for our own mistakes.

Instead, somebody else—hopefully with insurance—is responsible or accountable, but not you.

Maybe there is some providence at work here. When I got up this morning to work on this chapter, I flipped on the TV. The first advertisement went something like this, "Been involved in an accident? Whether or not it's your fault, call us because we can get money for *you*." Honorable leaders don't buy that. In fact, it works against everything they stand for.

There are several major takeaways from this chapter. The evidence is compelling that true dilemmas don't exist, or are very rare. Unfortunately, it is in our nature to engage in the R-word. The R-word is the world's largest manufacturer of artificial dilemmas and contrived complexity. To put this manufacturing out of business, honorable leaders often emphasize the simple or the basics. Simple and clear language, not unlike the West Point Honor Code, can help shape our attitudes and decisions. Also, you should now place in your arsenal the Three Rules of Thumb that help provide mental acuity as we approach various *moments* on our way to the high ground. I conclude this chapter by arguing that honorable leaders don't seek excuses, they seek responsibility. And they welcome the idea of accountability.

> *Honorable leaders don't search for excuses. Instead, they search for more responsibility. They want to be held accountable for their decisions and actions.*

Let's not stop here. Let's continue our advance to the high ground by Being Big About Small Things.

4

Be Big About Small Things

Every violation of the truth is not only a sort of suicide in the liar, but is a stab at the health of human society.

—Ralph Waldo Emerson

ARE YOU BIG ABOUT SMALL THINGS?

Major Fernando "Nando" Miguel is. With a Masters Degree in applied math and operations research and a promising career as an army aviator, Nando, at the time of our interview, had just finished his first year of teaching math at West Point. I was lucky enough to catch up with him during the summer break when I asked him about honor and its role in shaping leaders.

"I learned here, more than 10 years ago, that everything matters."

"What do you mean? Can you give me an example?" I asked.

"It's easy. It happened early on. In my formative years here."

He leaned back in his chair and cupped his hands behind his head and stared at some imaginary point on the ceiling. He began slowly.

"It was my team leader at the time. He was a yearling, you know a college sophomore. And I was his plebe. I was supposed to look up to this guy. He was my first ever front line supervisor, if you will."

"What happened, Nando?"

Well, my team leader was the source of it all. He went to the Physics department and there were solutions posted there to help everybody with their homework. He wasn't finished copying, and it says clearly on the front of the solution book in big, bold letters, "DO NOT TAKE FROM HERE." Well, he took the notebook full of homework solutions. Obviously, you're not supposed to do that.

Other cadets needed to get the solutions, but he took the notebook out of the physics department anyway. He brought it back to the barracks and shared it with some of his classmates. Mind you, it says on the cover, "DO NOT TAKE FROM HERE." Seven yearlings, or sophomores, got caught with the physics solution notebook and all seven were found for violating the Honor Code because they stole. Shortly thereafter, all seven resigned.

Consider a more recent example brought to me by a senior faculty member.

Each cadet company area has a single printer. And all 120 or so cadets can share this printer. Well, this young man that I mentor made a *big* mistake. He printed off too much stuff on this communal printer and you can't do that for large documents. But he printed off a ton of stuff anyway and he walked into the printer room to get it all and there were three other cadets in there. And everybody starts saying to this guy, "Hey, man, you've printed off more than the allowable pages." But this guy denies it saying that it isn't his. All three cadets then say to him, "Are you sure that isn't yours?" He denies it again. A couple hours later, he admitted he lied about this print job. He was found for violating the Honor Code for lying, but he was not separated from the academy. Rather, he was accepted for the honor mentorship program, and I was his mentor.

A couple of days after hearing about this case, I learned another from a young man who was just about to start his senior year.

Well, this case involves one of my old plebes. He moved out of my company after his plebe year. When he got to his new company as a yearling or sophomore, somebody sent out an e-mail to the entire new set of yearlings and said how they needed to shape up pretty much and that they weren't doing their job. Basically, critiquing the leadership abilities of this new group of yearlings. Well, my old plebe forwarded this e-mail to higher leadership. I think it was to the first sergeant and the company commander. But before he forwarded it, he changed around a couple of the words and what the guy said. Essentially, he first changed the text and then forwarded the e-mail on. These new words changed the meaning of the e-mail and made it sound more derogatory than it initially was. This guy was found guilty under our Honor Code for lying. He was not separated, though. He was turned back a year and will not graduate with his original class.

Now you might be wondering, "What's the big deal with all of this little stuff?" Or you may ask, "Who really cares about stupid little things such as hotel stacking, fake IDs, taking a solution manual from a physics department, lying about how much you print off on a printer, or taking the liberty to change another's text in an e-mail before sending it out?"

When you look over those who *do* lead from the high ground, you notice a characteristic that is conspicuously absent from those who lead from the low ground. Notably, honorable leaders care as much about the little as they do for the big. I refer to this as Being Big About Small Things. The three cases that start this chapter illustrate exactly this point.

This is a defining characteristic of honorable leadership and it is critical to BE BIG ABOUT SMALL THINGS to secure the high ground. If you want all the competitive advantages associated with leading from the high ground, you must begin with the small.

THE LAND OF OPPORTUNITY

Axial coding is a qualitative research process in which every sentence and every paragraph of all interviews and documents are scrutinized to capture main themes. Once these themes are captured, they are labeled and then compared against each other to detect patterns or consistencies.

It was during this time-consuming process that I arrived at a powerful conclusion. Namely, honorable leaders rely on "small" decision points to prepare for the "big." In fact, during some instances, I found that honorable leaders actually attempt to artificially inflate the "small" in preparation for the "big."

Nowhere is this more evident than in a conversation I had with infantry Lieutenant Colonel Brian Mennes. The issue was temptation.

I began, "How do you limit or remove the amount of temptation that these young leaders face?"

He set his steely stare upon me. He knew I had missed the mark.

"We don't limit. We expand," he responded.

"What?"

"This is about *more* temptation. Not less. Temptation is a good thing. The Superintendent wants more temptation for our leaders here, not less. He wants more decision-points."

Compare his remark to recent trends to control or constrain. Take, for instance, the Sarbanes-Oxley Act. The fundamental drive behind this piece of legislation is to enact safeguards, control mechanisms, and rules for corporate accountability. A compliance strategy such as this rarely serves to develop honorable leaders. Rather, its purpose is to prevent dishonorable leadership. Basically, controls such as Sarbanes-Oxley attempt to remove, not encourage temptation.

Using Sarbanes-Oxley as an exemplar, let's look at some of the facts behind this control mechanism. Since the passage of the Sarbanes-Oxley Act in 2002, most publicly traded firms have seen their audit costs skyrocket. For instance, Advanced Micro Devices pays in excess of $10.5 million annually in audit and audit-related expenses. The auditing cost increase for Advanced Micro Devices *pre* versus *post* Sarbanes-Oxley? A whopping 210 percent. A *USA Today* analysis of an AuditAnalytics.com data set indicates a 40 percent increase in 2004 audit and related fees for the S&P 500. The cost for compliance among the S&P's 500 companies? $3.5 billion![1]

Alan Cohen, CEO of shoe retailer Finish Line, says that one penny of every stock share goes to auditing fees and related expenses. Staples CEO

Ron Sargent strikes a common chord regarding Sarbanes-Oxley when he says that this legislation is "an overreaction" and that while "transparency is valuable, you can't legislate morality. If someone is determined to commit fraud, it could be done with or without legislation."[2] Intrigued by this last statement, I set out to do my own research into the efficacy of legislation and controls.

It appears that Ron Sargent's point is a valid one. In support of his claim is a rash of legislation and court decisions from the early 1990s intended to meet goals similar to what Sarbanes-Oxley attempts to meet now. Specifically, the 1991 Federal Sentencing Guidelines for Organizations was enacted to deter dishonorable leadership through a system of heavy fines and probation conditions. In addition to these guidelines, landmark court cases such as the 1996 *Caremark* decision provided a serious warning to key executives and corporate directors that they could be held personally liable for the corrupt behavior of their organizations. Ask yourself if these previous controls were effective at preventing Enron? WorldCom? Arthur Anderson? Adelphia? Boeing? Or TYCO?

Not satisfied with this level of analysis, I explored what top-tier empirical research had to say about this issue of compliance and controls. My investigation led me to one of the most cited empirical articles in contemporary management research. This article entitled "Effects of Human Resource Systems on Manufacturing Performance and Turnover" was written by a Cornell-trained business scholar, Jeffrey Arthur.[3] Professor Arthur identified two general types of human resource (HR) management systems, which he distinguished as either *commitment* or *control* programs. With a large sample of steel minimills, he examined the correlation between type of HR system and performance

> *Honorable leaders will always prefer commitment and leadership development strategies to compliance mechanisms.*

of the minimill. In his sample, mills with commitment systems were significantly more productive, had lower scrap rates, and lower employee turnover. In short, commitment trumped control. This supports one of my key observations—honorable leaders always prefer commitment to compliance.

Control Freak

Let's summarize the key points as they relate to controls, compliance, and sanction as a means to reach the high ground. First and foremost is the sheer expense of an over-reliance on control mechanisms. The Sarbanes-Oxley example illustrates this. Even at West Point, the costs of control and sanction are prohibitive. I talked to several cadets about the enforcement process of their Honor Code system. These young men and women affirmed the issue of cost as they detailed the loss of time and cognitive energy spent during investigations, the honor hearing, and the sentencing stage of the honor system process. John Winn, a former West Point law professor, expressed the costs of controls and, in particular, litigation aimed at removing temptation: "Litigation and contract enforcement is akin to being in the world's most expensive taxi cab. Add to that, you're in Manhattan traffic and there's a traffic jam. On top of all that, imagine that Donald Trump is your taxi driver. It is that *expensive*."

Second and closely related is that an over-reliance on controls is downright inefficient. Take for example the cases of Martha Stewart in 2004 and Bernie Ebbers of WorldCom in 2005. Ask yourself if these cases really move honorable leadership forward. Probably not.

Instead, the emphasis here is on the punitive approach to fixing dishonorable leadership. By its very nature, strategies like this don't focus on honorable leadership. Rather, these approaches punish *dis*honorable leadership. Furthermore, controls and punitive measures are always reactive. Put differently, they go into effect after the damage has already occurred to others, such as a firm's shareholders. Staying with WorldCom, we can see the catastrophic loss in jobs and in financial investments that arise from this reactive approach to building honor.

Consider the case of Qwest Communications. Qwest inflated revenue statements by using network capacity "swaps" and improper accounting techniques as they related to long-term deals and investments. Qwest admitted in an internal audit review that it incorrectly accounted for and, in the process, inflated $1.16 billion in sales. Accordingly, they restated results for years 2000, 2001, and 2002.[4] In 2002, the SEC mandated that Qwest pay $250 million to defrauded investors. That was the easy part. The tough part has been the inefficient process of tracking down any, and all, investors in Qwest. Even by conservative estimates, less than 2 cents of every dollar has

> *Control mechanisms aimed at removing leader temptation rarely work as expected. Generally, they are inefficient and expensive.*

been returned to investors. We begin to see how expensive and inefficient compliance and control mechanisms really are.

CC Me on That!

This is not to say that West Point shuns controls. Because, they don't. I found, however, that the real point of departure for honorable leaders and organizations is how they integrate and balance the "control" approach with their "commitment"-oriented strategy to develop leaders. To honorable leaders, control strategies have their place, but they often take a backseat to more developmental or commitment-oriented leadership strategies.

Sanction, in the form of honor hearings, is never the first or preferred choice of the honorable leaders at West Point. Honorable leaders, however, understand that controls and sanctions are an essential part of leadership and effective operations. Indeed, West Point must have them to show a consequence for both big and small decisions. The opening cases do illustrate that honorable leaders tend to apply sanction even-handedly to both the big and small. Indeed, in the first case, we saw seven young leaders resign in the face of certain separation. Understand that at West Point the penalty would've been exactly the same if the cadets had stolen $1000 from another's room or had lied to the dean of students. Whether big or small, control mechanisms help deliver a consequence for a leader's decisions and behavior.

With that said, I still saw Dave Jones of the Simon Center for the Professional Military Ethic actually wince when we discussed the verdicts on some of the more recent honor cases. After several meetings with Dave Jones, I better understood his reaction. When controls, fines, or sanctions are exercised, they are really an outward manifestation of failure. Use of controls demonstrates a failure in the commitment-oriented approach and in the developmental approach to building honorable leaders. That's why Dave Jones and other honorable leaders used the number of young men and women found for violating the West Point Honor Code as a diagnostic tool, or a barometer of the effectiveness of their commitment strategy.

When honor cases surge at West Point, they don't look to increase the number or severity of controls. Instead, they know that their leadership development process is not working. Accordingly, they look to their leadership and training development program as the source of improvement. And this is the key point of departure that separates honorable leaders and honorable organizations from all others. And this is where temptation is again critical to growing honorable leaders.

> When the use of controls and punishment increases, we know that we are neglecting the leadership development process.

Advance or Retreat?

In the face of expensive and punitive controls, the natural response is retreat. Fear leads to leadership paralysis. Fear of litigation, fear of contracts, and fear of not complying. When the stakes are high, those leading from the low ground abandon their commitment and development processes. One powerful way to exterminate temptation and remove *moments* is to centralize decision-making. Of course, when leaders or organizations move in this direction, they also eradicate empowerment, and junior leaders become stale. Under this scenario, leaders aren't developed.

I can draw on a personal example that illustrates this idea. My first job after I left the army as an intelligence officer was that of a junior manager for Corning. I worked in a large, optical fiber plant in Wilmington, North Carolina. After 11 months, I left Corning. It was not because of my peer group because they were fun and smart. It was not because of my employees who were hard working and conscientious. It was not because of the product. Optical fiber is one of the greatest inventions of the last 2000 years.

To me, it boiled down to lack of discretion, that is, no opportunity to be tested; to grow. Like many organizations, Corning feared its union, feared the Occupational Health and Safety Organization (OSHA), and feared Wall Street. Driven by that fear, they tried to eradicate what they thought were decision-making "mistakes." Consequently, they centralized decision-making to a few executives at the upper echelons of the plant. Not only was this an inefficient and slow way of managing, it is the antithesis of leading. When leaders cannot make decisions, they are no longer leaders.

> *Without facing moments, a leader cannot lead.*

The irony of this is with the attempt to limit or restrain decision-making coupled with the fear of sanction, smart people become bored and they become mischievous. Because it's impossible to eradicate all managerial discretion, people without practice actually make many more mistakes with much fewer opportunities. Without any tempting *moments* found in commitment

> *When you remove temptation and moments, things will always get worse, never better.*

or development leadership programs, the ratio of poor decisions to *moments* will actually increase and the use of controls and sanctions will actually multiply.

My research at West Point overwhelmingly confirmed this point. Despite the constant Congressional oversight and the severity of sanctions both at the organizational level (e.g., reduced federal budgets) and at the individual level (e.g., separation and dismissal from the academy), West Point sought to minimize their reliance on controls by maximizing *moments*. What I mean by this is that honor-

> *For leadership and organizational growth to occur, there must be as many moments (big and small) as possible.*

able leaders want more temptation, more *moments*, more discretion, and more opportunities to be tested. I reached the conclusion that retreat will never secure the high ground. You must grow and advance to secure the high ground. Honorable leaders wouldn't have it any other way.

To Secure the High Ground, Shun the Safe Harbor

This idea of maximizing little or small *moments* to minimize reliance on controls reminds me of a conversation I had with Donald Hatfield several years ago. Don is a business strategy professor at Virginia Tech. I approached him about choosing a dissertation topic for my doctorate. I could choose a topic that was relatively boring, but for which there was plenty of material and data. If I chose this option, I'd be done with my dissertation in a relatively short time, maybe a period of months. The other option involved a more exciting topic to me, but one that was under-researched and maybe not recognized by the business strategy community. Our conversation went something like this.

I started, "Dr. Hatfield, which one do you think I should go with."

"Do you like my picture?"

"What? What are you talking about?" I snapped.

"That one." He pointed behind him and there was a picture of a sailboat in a nice quiet bay. It wasn't the busy Sydney Harbor. It was a quiet quay, maybe in the Caribbean somewhere. St. John, perhaps.

I dismissed it impatiently, "Yeah, it's fine. Let's get back to the question at hand. Please, Dr. Hatfield."

"You really didn't look at my picture. I hate it."

"You what?"

"I hate it. Harbors are too safe. Once you find the safe haven of a harbor, you never want to leave. But that's never good. You never get tested. You don't experience the elements. What kind of sailor could you be, if you never left the harbor?"

"Uhhh. Not a good one."

"That's right. It's boring and you're never put to the test. Your mettle is never tested. To find what you're made of, you must have the courage to leave the harbor. Okay, enough about this stupid little picture. Let's talk about your options here."

There wasn't a need. He made his point. I chose to leave the harbor.

Talking sailing ships and rough green oceans with my professor brought to mind the short story, "Youth: A Narrative," by Polish-born, British novelist Joseph Conrad who spent half his life at sea, much of it during the last of the era of iron men on wooden ships under sail. Writing in 1902 about surviving a vicious Atlantic gale in 1877 when he was only 20, Conrad recalled, "I did not know how good a man I was till then." So, too, with navigating dangerous *moments* and surviving with one's honor unscratched.

Move back to *moments* for a second. Earlier I compared these to an intersection. Now, suppose that you were given a chance to drive across America. There are two strategies that you would consider.

The first is what I'll call the interstate strategy. Here, you would get on Interstate 80 around Newark. You'd never have to get off I-80 and, presto, 2300 miles later, you'd empty out on the Pacific Ocean around San Fran. If you didn't like I-80 through the Rust Belt, you could get on I-40 in Wilmington, North Carolina, and stay on I-40 until you reached Bakersfield, California. What could be easier? No intersections. At least 70 mph, not a lot of thinking. Every 200 miles or so, you could pull off and eat at a Cracker Barrel, or at Applebee's. You'd never want for a place to stay. Inns of all sorts, Holiday, DAYS, Hampton, all dot our highway system. But assuming you had enough time, would you really want to go this way? Would you really get to see America as it really is? Would you grow? Have memories that would last? Probably not.

I wouldn't. I'd go with option Two. I would take roads like State Routes 11, 422, 3, or 24 through such places as Great Falls, North Carolina; Dahlonega, Georgia; Lexington, Virginia; Truth or Consequences, New Mexico; Hurricane, Utah, or Kennewick, Washington. There'd be fewer Applebee's, but many more intersections. Small intersections, but more character. Different people. Diverse country. More and better memories. And plenty of personal growth.

Consider the closing words of Robert Frost's famous poem, "The Road Less Traveled."

> Two roads diverged in a wood, and I—
> I took the one less traveled by,
> And that has made all the difference

These two metaphors of harbors and interstates both conform to a belief firmly rooted by those on the high ground. I found that honorable leaders shun the safety of the harbor. They want to be tested. They want to test others. In addition, honorable leaders refuse the Interstate. They prefer as many *moments* or intersections as possible—both big and small. To them, that is how they grow and learn to be honorable leaders. Reaching the high ground is not about personal safety. Just the opposite; it's about exposing yourself and your team to repeated risks and tests.

> *To be truly BIG ABOUT SMALL THINGS, you must have the courage and the desire to face as many moments as possible.*

BUILD YOUR BACKBONE

One night during the summer, I caught up with a young man named John who was just returning to West Point after summer leave. On the following day, he would begin Army Air Assault School. This is the type of training you see on the U.S. Army commercials with soldiers repelling from a helicopter.

We talked over a bowl of spaghetti and we were away from any of his superiors.

I started, "Did you cheat in high school?"

Without pause John snapped, "Yeah, I did. Not a lot. But I did."

I conducted some research and found this fact not unusual. In a recent survey of *High School Who's Who* winners, 80 percent of them admitted to cheating.

I pressed, "Have you cheated here?"

"No."

Curious I asked, "How can you explain that?"

"Well. First, when I got here, I was tempted. And to be totally truthful, I thought about it early on. This place may be the most competitive place on earth. You never want to be last. *I* didn't want to be last."

"What stopped you?"

"It's kind of crazy, but, at first, it was fear. Fear of getting caught and fear of getting kicked out. But then things changed."

"How so?"

"I just don't think about it anymore."

"Think about what?" I asked.

"Well, I don't think of cheating and I'm not afraid of getting kicked out. I am a junior now and I've moved on. There were so many opportunities to cheat, lie, and even steal. Do you know most people don't lock their doors here?"

I nodded.

"The first real opportunity that comes to mind was when my psychology professor left me alone to take a make-up exam. I didn't study as much as I should've. I wanted to cheat. I could've cheated. I was a plebe. Thought about it hard. Actually, put down my pencil. Was really tempted to pull out my notes. But I didn't. I guess this is silly, but to me, it's really about confidence. After I made it through the first little temptation, the second, the third, the thirtieth, the fiftieth, the hundredth, I could feel myself getting stronger. Now, after being here for two years, I guess I'm on my five thousandth temptation!" he laughs. "But now, I don't even think twice about it. I'm just more confident. Can you pass the Parmesan cheese?"

"Yeah."

During a research meeting, I continually returned to this conversation with this young man. It became apparent to me through my interview with John that he possessed something special, what I call a strong honor backbone. But it wasn't always that way. And this is probably true for all of our backbones. At birth, our backbones are pliable and the surrounding muscles are undeveloped. We know, however, that they can get stronger with practice, with use. We see this play out with John. As he successfully navigated each and every *moment*, his honor backbone grew stronger.

One cannot overstate the importance of this last point. The best weightlifters in the world, who, by the way, rely on the strength of their backbones, will tell you that they just didn't wake up one morning and bench press 500 pounds. It all begins with mastering the smaller weights, the little weights, first. Take, for instance, Anthony Ricciuto, who was the Drug-Free World deadlifting champion. In 1992, Anthony set a Drug-Free Teenage World record in the deadlift of 500 pounds in the 220-pound weight class. Imagine how much practice, how many smaller weights Anthony had to lift before reaching the 500-pound barrier. Quite simply, to be BIG Anthony and John both had to begin with the SMALL before moving up.

The case of Anthony Ricciuto and my conversation with John reflect a simple truth of honorable leadership: Your honor is tested on the little, but is revealed in the big.

Redefine "Defining Moments"

As part of my research, I examined several magazine articles and book titles that emphasized the notion of "defining moments." More often than not, these defining moments were described as "the penultimate victory," "the colossal crisis," "averting disaster," "delivering when the chips are down," "executing at the eleventh hour," or "doing your best when the world is watching." The assumption behind this language is that your leadership is tested in the big crises. I found something quite different when I talked to honorable leaders.

My evidence indicates that honorable leaders actually *redefine* "defining moments." To them, "defining moments" are not some grand spectacle where you rise up to save the day. In contrast, honorable leaders see "defining moments" more humbly, more quietly. Brian Mennes put it best when he indicated that the first place to test somebody is never on the big. Rather, test them on the small, on the little, to help them prepare for the big. Falling back to the idea of physical training, can you really expect somebody to show up at an event and automatically run a 5-minute mile or hoist 500 pounds without any training? Of course not, and I found that the same truth that applies to the physical world also relates to our leadership development. Honorable leaders don't jump into the big or force somebody else into the big without first providing them as many *moments* as possible to practice.

Suppose for a moment that you do engage in heavy lifting, without stretching or without practice. More than likely, you will overreach and your backbone can become strained. In the worst case, the backbone could break. But even a simple strain affects the entire body, reducing its capacity to do work, to accomplish goals, and to lead effectively.

It's important to understand that making it to the high ground and navigating the big *moments* are never luxuries of circumstance. The honorable leaders whom I interviewed clearly arrived there through a strong backbone

> *Your honor backbone is built and tested on the small, but is revealed on the BIG.*

built through repeated practice. In a sense, the honorable leaders are not entirely unlike George Mallory and Andrew Irvine, the climbers who were among the first to scale Mount Everest. In both cases, strong backs are necessary to carry your arsenal of tools. And, occasionally, to carry others to the summit.

THE REFLEX

My interview with John exhibits another core characteristic that I found in numerous other honorable leaders. In most cases, those who lead from the high ground possess what I call an *honor reflex*.

The number one indicator of this honor reflex is an almost involuntary or automatic response to *moments*. Unlike a true muscle reflex such as a sneeze, blink, or hiccup, this is a *learned* reflex. We know from prior discussion that this learned reflex is built through practice and exposure to moments. In several cases, I noticed a gradual transition from labored, overly cautious, and concerned thinking as one approaches a *moment* to a more intuitive, reflexive response.

We can see this in the case of John. Initially, he felt tempted to cheat. Apparently, he invested significant cognitive energy and self-restraint to pull back at the last minute when it came to cheating on his psychology exam. Later, however, he learned to breeze through *moments* in a safe and expeditious fashion. Again, the ability to accomplish this seems rooted in continuous practice.

After I collected all of the interview data, I detected a similar difference among West Point classes. Plebes or freshmen seemed to struggle at times with the most elemental *moments*. Dave Jones affirmed this. Most lapses of honor typically happen during the initial 6 to 12 months at West Point. Young men and women enter West Point from all parts of the country and from all levels of society. Not surprisingly, some come with different and diverse value sets. Many young men and women falter because they haven't had enough practice or intersections to hone their decision-making skills. Again, my interview with John is clear evidence of this fact.

Compare West Point seniors. Many of those whom I interviewed demonstrated what I'll call *requisite depth*. For "easy" intersections, they allocated exactly the right amount of cognitive energy, which was usually quite small, to navigate the *moment*. Conversely, when they were exposed to true dilemmas, they used the requisite depth to deal with this more complicated and dangerous *moment* or intersection.

The beauty of requisite depth is that efficiency and effectiveness interact. When the *moment* is relatively straightforward, honorable leaders don't delay. They quickly navigate the intersection with their honor intact. On the other hand, during more difficult decision-making points, leaders on the high ground exercise more caution.

The honor reflex enables leaders to act correctly and decisively. Since many of the issues we face are not true dilemmas, this honor reflex provides a direct competitive advantage to those who can build this reflex. While others ponder over a relatively simple *moment*, the honorable leader uses this reflex to quickly move from this easier *moment* to more difficult and challenging issues. The leaders without it are still stuck in first gear.

When I examine honorable leaders, I found this notion of requisite depth of critical importance. It is important to note that these leaders recognize the extreme danger of applying the honor reflex to a dangerous and complex moment—a true dilemma. Thus, not only must honorable leaders build their

> *Build your honor reflex to make it through most moments; never use your honor reflex during true dilemmas.*

honor reflex, they tend to exercise it instinctively in only those *moments* that demand it.

TRADING UP

In keeping with my fascination with the interstate, intersection, and driving theme, I compared the development of honorable leaders to the idea of trading up to buy a car.

At first, many of the novice leaders at West Point, the freshmen, seemed to be Yugos. They were driving in a slow, rather primitive, vehicle. It was enough, however, to make it through the intersections. It just took more effort and taxed their engines to a greater degree. As these young men and women grew, I saw them move from a Yugo to a Pontiac to a Chrysler 300M to a BMW 700 series. At the highest levels, they were more nimble, flexible, but still safe, in making it through all kinds of intersections—both the big and the little ones.

When Millions become Billions

Recall that I argue that from the highest elevations, you can see both near and far. In classic honorable leadership style, I found this to be the case when leaders make such a big deal about issues that most others would ignore or dismiss. The honorable leaders whom I witnessed tended to immediately recognize that if you don't deal with the small, you are bound to face the big.

This is important since leaders confront challenges and solve problems. Among those who lead from the high ground, there is a preference to intervene early before a problem snowballs into an overly complex, expensive, and complicated debacle.

Upon further investigation, I found this notion based on one of two similar premises. The first is that a single little action can explode into something bigger and harder to manage. The second premise is related to the prior point, but distinct. Honorable leaders seem to understand that even if a single small problem doesn't explode into a big one, little problems, by themselves, can add up. I was intrigued by these assumptions so I did my own research to test the veracity of these claims.

These assumptions appear to hold. Consider the following facts. Approximately $50 billion dollars every year is lost to employee theft. Moreover, national surveys estimate that 75 percent of all employees steal from their employers at least once in their careers. That number seemed awfully high to me so I sought out other data to help validate this claim. The 15th Annual Retail Theft Survey of 2002 conducted by Jack L. Hayes International, a loss prevention consulting firm, found that $4.7 billion was lost to shoplifting and employee theft in twenty-five major, U.S. retail companies. This was not one or two people stealing billions at a time. Rather, it was thousands of people stealing dollars at a time. It is not the scope of a single act that is important. Instead, it is the volume of many small acts that is destructive.

Honorable leaders seem to implicitly understand what is reinforced by these staggering numbers. When little effects or problems go unnoticed, undetected, or ignored, they can accumulate into a much larger effect.

| Little things add up! |

I present the case of Bristol-Myers-Squibb (BMS) as evidence that a single little act, in and by itself, can snowball. This is a classic case where millions became billions. I personally discussed this issue with a senior level manager at BMS whose son just finished his plebe year at West Point.

Beginning around 2000, BMS apparently felt pressure to hit internal and external sales and earnings numbers. Realizing that they weren't going to make it, some senior leaders at BMS searched for a quick fix. The scheme that the CFO and other high-profile leaders launched is called "channel stuffing."

This involved offering extreme financial incentives to induce wholesalers to buy and hold a greater volume of prescription drugs—much more than consumer demand warranted. What began as a one-time practice ballooned from calendar quarter to quarter. By the end of 2001, this channel-stuffing scheme placed nearly $2 billion worth of excess, unused, and unneeded inventory at BMS's wholesalers. Of course, this resulted in an artificial inflation of sales and earnings. In addition, several key leaders signed SEC documents with omissions and misleading information regarding sales and earnings performance. To further conceal their channel stuffing, senior leaders used accounting and bookkeeping gimmicks to hide the wholesalers' huge inventory levels. To add insult to injury, the incentives to wholesalers cost BMS tens of millions of dollars.[5]

BMS paid $300 million to settle a federal prosecution on the charges of committing securities and exchange fraud. By conservative estimates, the cost of this problem, which began as a one-time "little" fix, approached $1 billion. This figure included a $100 million SEC civil penalty, a $50 million shareholder payment fund, the settling of two, large class-action lawsuits, and the endowment of a business ethics chair at Seton Hall University.

Honorable leaders are BIG ABOUT SMALL THINGS because they possess the awareness, courage, and discipline to intervene early to prevent small things from accumulating or from ballooning into a much more serious event.

In the long run, it spares pain and conserves resources to fix a problem early. Occasionally, at West Point this is done through separation from the academy—even on little issues. This is done in the rarest of cases. It is an article of faith that one day these young men and women will be in charge of saving and protecting lives and that

| BE BIG ABOUT SMALL THINGS to ensure those little moments never fester into tragic or expensive consequences. |

honorable leaders are best at accomplishing this. Keep in mind, however, that this is also done in the very best of private and public organizations. In

Jim Collins' book *Good to Great*, we learn that Level 5 leaders get the best people on the bus and cut their losses early when dealing with "the bad apples." Typically, West Point prefers feedback, mentoring, and rehabilitation as a proactive method to ensure that little *moments* never evolve into the scene of an accident at a much bigger and busier intersection.

HONEY, I SHRUNK THE...

After many years, in 2005, I finally gave in and took the family to Disney World in Orlando, Florida. Everyone was telling me that my girls, 6 and 8, were the perfect ages to fully enjoy the parks.

One of the more interesting Offstein Family episodes occurred during and just after we went to the *Honey, I Shrunk the Kids* movie set. Here, we put on our 3D glasses and sat through a rather impressive interactive movie. In one of the scenes, a laser from the screen was pointed at the audience and a blinding flash of light filled the theater—we were all zapped by Professor Szalinski's shrinking laser! In a clever twist, everything on the screen became very big, which had the effect of making the audience feel small.

At about this time, I turned down to my youngest, Molly, with her 3D glasses. I could see her tense; she was gripping the seat to the point that her elbows were shaking. Thankfully, Professor Szalinski fixed his laser and was able to return the audience to its normal size. As expected, there were cheers and whoops from the audience. It was all in good sport, or so I thought.

About 30 minutes later, we were standing in line for another ride when Molly gripped my hand and looked up at me.

"Dadda, that was nice of them to upsize us."

"What Molly?"

"You know, Dadda. We wouldn't be able to enjoy the park if they didn't upsize us back. We wouldn't even be able to ride this ride," she said as she pointed to a sign that said, "You must be 42 inches or higher."

I realized that either this was the deadpan moment of a lifetime or she really thought that she'd been shrunk. Of course, it was the latter. To Molly, for about 30 minutes she was 9 inches tall.

I tell this story only to colorfully illustrate a phenomenon that I observed in cases of dishonorable leadership. Interestingly, it is the R-word at work. In this case, however, the R-word does not transform the simple to the complex, but it transforms the big or medium into the small or microscopic.

Can you imagine people saying to themselves and to others, "It's no big deal," or "It's so small, who cares anyway," or maybe it's "What's one stolen song or pirated movie when Spielberg is making $300 million anyway; who's going to miss it?" In a sense, the R-word is like Professor Szalinski's laser. The

> *When you act BIG ABOUT SMALL THINGS, you make it difficult, if not impossible, to engage in the R-word.*

R-word is an artificial way to minimize the very things that we should care about, that we should address.

When honorable leaders act BIG ABOUT SMALL THINGS, they reverse this process.

> *Your ability to be BIG ABOUT SMALL THINGS improves your chances of being big when big things really occur.*

When honorable leaders act BIG ABOUT SMALL THINGS, they make it difficult to engage in the R-word. To those leading from the high ground, this is necessary for effective leadership. I uncovered a very strong belief consistently held by honorable leaders. Namely, they refuse to distinguish between a big and small breach of their honor. During my interviews, they would respond with a common refrain: "If you compromise your honor on a small issue, how can you *not* do it when the stakes are much higher."

LAW OF RELATIVITY

West Point's philosophy and that of those leading from the high ground is that you don't want to invest a lot of mental energy into distinguishing what is a small from what is a big breach of honor. They are also quick to point out the problems that surface from what I call the law of ethical relativity. What one considers small, another may consider big. You can picture the personal, team, and organizational problems when each and every person has their own take on what a small breach and what a large breach of honor is. Lying on an expense account may be "no big deal" to one, but a very big deal to another.

Move from the leadership to the management arena. From a production and operational standpoint, would you ever want an organization to have 5,000 different ideas on how to run the production line? The best of leaders and the best of organizations demand creativity and imagination. But in certain core processes, such as production or the workings of the supply chain, that just isn't the case. Clearly, Wal-Mart does not want much imagination or creativity in their distribution process. I found that honorable leaders do not want different ideas of what "right" is or what "wrong" is within their organization. You avoid this when you treat the big and little the same.

The Worst Is Yet to Come

It also began to dawn on me that a pervasive sentiment among honorable leaders is the special symbolic nature of the little things. Many of the leaders that I interviewed inside and outside West Point clearly felt that, if you tolerate a little breach, then you are implicitly stating that "It's Okay to do worse." When leaders ignore, dismiss, or tolerate small breaches, they are giving up ground, retreating.

A leadership trend that I detected in honorable leaders is an understanding or a premonition that the small *will* turn into the big. Notice the language here. It is not a question of *if*, it is a question of *when*. This is different from all others who say to themselves the small WILL NOT turn into the big. Or that the small is very unlikely to turn into the big. The case with Bristol-Myers-Squibb proves this point. It was going to be a one-time ordeal. I can imagine them using the R-word to say, "Just once. This'll never go on. Just this one time."

Contrast those sentiments with the feelings of a young man I interviewed during the summer of 2005.

No matter what, in the back of my head I am thinking, "You know what, I remember on leave one time he lied to some bartender about his age just to get a beer. If he'll do that, I bet something similar will happen if I need to sign off on some supplies and he gives me a short account and then I'm holding a million dollar bag." So, it's always in the back of my head. No matter how big or how small, I will always wonder if he is going to help me later on in life, or is he going to stiff me on something.

Start Small and Finish Big

West Point is a fallible organization. Despite their over-the-top emphasis on honorable leadership, these junior leaders still occasionally lie, cheat, or steal. Leadership failures do exist at West Point. There are important caveats here, though. First among them is that leadership setbacks are a part of all organizations. However, what many leaders and organizations dismiss, ignore, or, are plainly unaware of, is rarely, if ever, overlooked by honorable leaders and the teams and organizations that they lead.

A large part of this chapter deals with just *having* these little *moments*. Honorable leaders ensure that this happens through a commitment-oriented leadership development process that can be characterized best as having:

- A high-performance environment
- Consequences for both the big and small lapses
- Plenty of feedback
- Decentralized decision-making.

This is where honorable leaders and organizations distinguish themselves from their competition. Where most ordinary managers revert to control mechanisms and the removal of tempting *moments*, honorable leaders do just the opposite. They recognize that the weak get weaker when they are given no opportunity to make decisions and lead. Conversely, the strong only get stronger with each passing *moment*.

Another major takeaway is the enormous expense of strict reliance on controls and when leaders fail to address the little things. Indeed, I provide specific and direct evidence that little things, if not addressed, can spiral out of control or just accumulate over time. I also uncovered a truth that is readily embraced by those on the high ground: Before you can master the big, you must master the small.

And that last sentence may be the most revealing and important line of this book. Whereas many books and several leadership theories contend that leaders are born, not made, this view flies in the face of what West Point and other honorable organizations and leaders stand for. These special organizations and leaders strongly believe that leaders aren't born, but are built over time. It's comforting to know that we all are capable of leading from the high ground through practice. Indeed, the journey to the summit begins with mastering several little steps. So what are you waiting for? Go forth and BE BIG ABOUT SMALL THINGS!

5

Go All In!

The chains which cramp us most are those which weigh on us least.
—Anne Sophie Swetchine

CHRIS MONEYMAKER KNOWS
HOW TO GO "ALL IN"

In 2003, Chris Moneymaker found himself sitting across the famed poker player, Sammy Farha, a Lebanese-born poker professional. ESPN poker analyst Norm Chad once referred to Farha as having the guts of a cat burglar. Farha seemed the odds-on favorite to win the $2.5 million purse at the World Series of Poker Championship. After all, Moneymaker was just an amateur. In fact, Moneymaker earned the $10,000 entry fee to the World Series of Poker by winning a $39 online satellite tournament.[1]

With cap pulled tightly over his brow and gazing at Farha through sunglasses, Moneymaker said, "I'm all in." In what is now considered one of the most historic heads-up matches in Texas Hold 'Em poker history, Moneymaker flopped his two pair, making a full house and easily crushed Farha's flopped pair of jacks. Moneymaker knew how to go "all in" and because of that he turned $39 into $2.5 million.

Within the context of the poker world, going all in is not to be taken lightly. Actually, this is the penultimate poker move. Going all in requires that the player devote all available resources, all chips, to his course of action. This decision to go all in requires an overwhelming commitment from the player—if she wins, she earns a big payday and stays to play. If she loses, when going all in, all chips disappear and the game is over for that player.

> *Going All In! reflects a 100 percent commitment to honorable leadership.*

It may seem blasphemous to discuss Texas Hold 'Em Poker in the same context as honorable leadership. But after interviewing honorable leaders at West Point and beyond, I kept returning to Chris Moneymaker and this concept of going all in. To be true, a defining characteristic of honorable leaders is that they appear to *Go All In!* all of the time. Many are quick to point out that it is impossible to reach the high ground without a 100 percent commitment or, put differently, without *Going All In!*

24/7

A general finding across all samples of honorable leaders is that they refuse to compartmentalize leadership. Said differently, the practice of leadership does not stop after 5:00 P.M. or away from the office. The natural outgrowth of this perspective is the fact that honorable leaders do not distinguish between their personal and professional lives. To reach the high ground, individuals must demonstrate honorable leadership in their private and professional lives, in all settings and situations. To ascend to the high ground requires this *All In!* commitment. If you follow and believe in this approach, leadership no longer becomes a workday or public responsibility. Rather, it is something that is practiced 24 hours a day, 7 days a week, or "24/7."

This more comprehensive perspective of leadership boils back down to the BE. Remember, I first noted that to *do* good, we must first *be* good. The BE will always precede the do. This emphasis on the BE makes compartmentalizing or dividing leadership into private and work life impossible. I asked several West Point men and women how their practice of leadership differed between their lives at work, at home, or in the community. In almost every case, and after they examined me in a most quizzical fashion, I would always hear the same response. There is no, or very little, difference in how they lead. According to them, there is only one BE. It is who you are. When we act honorably in one arena, such as our professional lives, but not in another, we are violating a fundamental law of nature. It is difficult, and almost impossible, to lead two different and separate lives. That is why honorable leaders, by and large, believe that it is inconceivable to be an honorable leader at work, but not at home or in the community. The settings may change, but you don't. The BE remains.

> *When it comes to honorable leadership, those on the high ground don't distinguish between work and play.*

That's not to say that one can't lead if they do decide to separate how they lead in their professional and personal lives. However, to use a poker metaphor to reflect the feeling shared by many honorable leaders that I talked with—the odds are stacked heavily against you if you go this route.

Taking a 24/7 approach toward honorable leadership does not mean that an occasional slip in one area is going to permanently affect a leader in another. Returning for a second to military history, it is a fact that almost all of the battlefield ascents to the high ground have not been linear. Rather, there are some setbacks, some small retreats that are necessary to regroup and begin again the move up. Indeed, this could very well have been the case with Rudolph Giuliani. Lawyers

> *Honorable leaders don't have dual identities or separate lives.*

for Giuliani's estranged wife, Donna Hanover, said she was granted a divorce and a large settlement only after Giuliani admitted to "cruel and inhumane" treatment based on a relationship with another woman. Despite this setback, many recognize Giuliani as an honorable and courageous leader.[2] A 24/7 philosophy on honorable leadership understands and accounts for these slipups and setbacks. However, approaching leadership from a 24/7 angle acknowledges that what we do in one facet of our life always has the *potential* to impact another facet of a leader's life. Let's take a deeper look on why and how a 24/7 approach to honorable leadership may be more important today than at any other time in modern management history.

A quick and cursory examination of recent trends suggests a Perfect Storm brewing that may further separate honorable leaders with an *All In!*, 24/7 perspective from low elevation leaders who do not. One trend that influences this debate is the sheer abundance of information that exists about each and every one of us. Whereas 10, 15, or 20 years ago, it would've been difficult for an employee to know about the lives of their immediate supervisor, midmanager, or top leadership, it is easy, cheap, and fast to do so now. Just type your name into Google and see how much control you have over the information online about you. Thus, the common mantra that a "leader is always under a microscope" has never been more true since the visibility of leaders is accentuated by the amount of information about them now available.

Another notable trend is the blurring of work and play. More often than not, people are working harder and longer. Consequently, people do more work at home and conduct more private business at work. This, too, seems affected by technology. Many organizations expect their leaders to be easily accessible away from work via the phone, fax, beeper, e-mail, or BlackBerry. Thus, the once clear boundaries between personal and professional lives are almost completely eroded now. The ramification is that it is tough to determine where our professional lives end and our personal lives begin. Artificially breaking these aspects of our life into two parts can put a leader in a precarious position—others may see you in a professional situation when you see yourself in a private or personal one. This misunderstanding is less likely to arise when leaders strive to act with honor in all aspects of their lives.

The Feeling Is Mutual

In February 2004, Claire O'Connell attempted to enter the board meeting for MassMutual Financial Group to share an unpleasant message—she believed her husband, CEO Robert J. O'Connell, was having an affair with the firm's top female executive, Susan Alfano.[3]

Robert Ackerman, the one-time CEO of Corning, intercepted Ms. O'Connell before she could enter the boardroom. While Ms. O'Connell never was able to directly address the board, several people close to MassMutual suggest that this incident sparked an internal investigation that brought to light matters much worse. Only months after Ms. O'Connell attempted to barge into the boardroom, MassMutual directors voted unanimously to fire Mr. O'Connell. The rationale for doing so was not the alleged affair. Instead, investigations revealed that Mr. O'Connell's supplemental retirement account had exploded to over $30 million dollars. Of particular note, the individual charged with overseeing and managing this account was his suspected lover, Susan Alfano. Also brought to the board's attention during the investigation was Mr. O'Connell's improper purchase of a Florida condominium from MassMutual at a ridiculously discounted price along with frequent use of corporate aircraft for what seemed solely personal use. Mr. O'Connell also appeared to hire several members of his own family at MassMutual who were neither fully qualified nor had requisite experience for their positions.

Using the events that occurred at MassMutual as a mini case study, we can see some of the potential problems that accompany 9-to-5 leadership compared to the 24/7, *All In!* approach.

One aspect of this case that may be overlooked is the sheer inefficiency of leading a double life. MassMutual's O'Connell had been the CEO for several years and the company had performed favorably despite some of the dubious events occurring in his personal life. It appears that Mr. O'Connell pretended to be honorable, but his other actions within and just outside the boundaries of MassMutual suggest otherwise. The idea of acting one way in one facet of life while acting differently in another is rooted in the assumption that a leader can hide or prevent information from leaking or bleeding from one sector to another. We've already noted how difficult this is to do in a technology-rich and information-heavy environment. Hence, for Mr. O'Connell, the question never was going to be *if* the information about the affair, ballooning retirement account, or below-market-value condominium was going to get out, the question was *when* it would get out. To get a good gauge of how inefficient and costly 9-to-5 leadership can be, imagine the activities of the top management team and directors during the first half of 2004 at MassMutual. Instead of the CEO and the board of directors of MassMutual concentrating on a competitive strategy during this time, it is likely they spent resources engaged in inefficient activities such as investigations, meetings, or contractual hearings. This unfortunate event is less likely

> *Leading from the high ground is not an act; it is a way of life.*

to happen to those that lead from the high ground because they don't lead double lives. They don't act or pretend. Quite simply, they are who they are.

Another closely related aspect of this case, is that it is difficult, if not impossible, to put on an act forever. Think back a second to the poker metaphor. Poker is a game of probabilities and percentages; it is less luck than you think. It is precisely these probabilities and percentages that make a total separation of personal and professional lives untenable. If a leader leads others dishonorably or by manipulation and deceit in their personal life, the probability that he will do the same in his professional life is quite high. Conversely, the odds can work in the opposite direction—if a leader acts with honor *away* from the public, it is more likely and easier to believe that she will lead honorably while *in* public or at the workplace.

Mixed Messages

Lieutenant Colonel Jeffrey Wilson became more than just a person to interview; he also became a friend and neighbor during my month-long residence at West Point in the summer of 2005. He best captured the importance of the *All In!*, 24/7 approach to leadership through a story he told.

> It was right after the Gulf War and we had this lieutenant colonel and I was a captain at the time and the Japanese Army wanted to know how we did it all logistically in Desert Storm. So this lieutenant colonel took two army captains, both of whom were two very good friends of mine, to Japan with him to brief the Japanese Defense Force on some of the things we had done in Desert Storm as part of the 24th Infantry Division. And while he was over there, he got totally wasted and went out to strip clubs and got Geisha girls to the point that he actually missed a meeting. The two captains showed up at the right place at the right time and he wasn't there. So then the two captains had to find him and then try to explain to the Japanese because there's the whole respect thing over there in Japan.

It is easy to grasp the immediate impact of this behavior and it relates directly to the discussion above—leading dishonorably outside work will eventually affect how one performs while at work. We can see here that what this lieutenant colonel did in his off hours had a dramatic and negative impact on his ability to lead and get work done from 9 to 5 while in Japan.

But, to fully understand and more deeply appreciate the impact of this leader's action, we need to look way beyond a single missed meeting. Jeff Wilson explained that this leader's future, his capacity to lead, was gone. "When he got back, of course, everybody knew what had happened. He couldn't do a single thing. He was totally ineffective. Nobody could take him seriously anymore. A couple nights of poor decisions in Japan were enough to really diminish his credibility as an administrator, leader, or authority figure."

Kevin Govern, another lieutenant colonel and a Marquette and Notre Dame graduate, adds to this sentiment: "If I make bad choices in my personal life....Well, that degrades my opportunity, my strength, to make the

> *When we Go All In! with honorable leadership, we increase our capacity to manage, influence, administer, and lead.*

right choices in life or death situations or it might undermine my reputation and esteem when the time comes for somebody picking and choosing to put me into command or into a position to be counted on."

My other interviews with honorable leaders seemed to echo what Govern and Wilson argued. And when I closely examined the text and listened again to the interviews, I detected a subtle attribute inherent to this *All In!*, 24/7 leadership philosophy. Notably, either through intuition or wisdom, honorable leaders seem to be able to see leadership through the eyes of both the leader and of the led.

Reduced to its atomic form, there are really three ways to actually "look" at leadership.

- *The first vantage is how leaders perceive themselves.* Most leaders do assess their own ability to lead. The big problem here is the self-attribution error—we tend to over-inflate how we actually perform as leaders. We're biased against negative evaluations of ourselves and our leadership abilities. Thus, this inward evaluation, while important, is not always accurate.

- *The second vantage is how others perceive us as leaders.* Another way to think of this is the audience reaction to our leadership performance. Sometimes the audience can be cruel and sometimes it, too, can be wrong. But whereas, we can easily fool ourselves, it is much more difficult to fool many.

- *The third vantage is the way we actually are.* This is difficult to nail down since much ado about leadership involves perception. But it is important to raise this point. Some leaders are good and honorable but suffer from a perception problem. This is not often the case, however, so I'd like to focus on the first two points here.

When I compare and contrast those who lead from the high ground and those who do not, a key difference emerges. Low elevation leaders tend to think almost exclusively from perspective One. These lower elevation leaders are more apt to separate their professional and personal behaviors because they value their own perception of their behavior above all else. In contrast, honorable leaders on the high ground seem to strike a balance between the first two perspectives. While they do self-assess their own behavior, they are also able to view their own leadership performance from the eyes, minds, and hearts of those they lead. These leaders seem to understand that acting one way at work while behaving differently off hours contributes to perceptions of hypocrisy. Think, for a moment, of the person you most respect and admire. I'd wager that they didn't abandon their honor or leadership duties when they clocked out of the office. No, we tend to respect and hold in the highest esteem those who act honorably regardless of place or time.

In one of the more interesting cross-cultural studies, a researcher named Andre Laurent asked a large and diverse sample to either agree or disagree with the following statement, "Through their professional activity, managers play an important role in society." Seventy-six percent of the French sample agreed. Seventy-four percent of Italians agreed. Sixty-five percent of Swiss agreed. And over half of all Americans agreed.[4] This provides some confirmation that others view managers and leaders in a much broader and wider context. A key point here is that leaders should never view themselves as off-duty because those whom they lead rarely do. To those we lead, we're always on duty. Honorable leaders sense and embrace, not shun, this 24/7 leadership perspective.

> *A 24/7, All In! approach presents to all a consistent and positive message.*

One of the fundamental biological imperatives within all of us is the psychological need to make sense of our world and our surroundings. This is much more difficult to do when we face inconsistencies. Honorable leaders understand this point and attempt to lead from the high ground in every aspect of their lives. No doubt, it's not easy. But going *All In!* never is. And that is what makes the high ground such a special place—it is hard to get to and not everybody can. Indeed, not everybody wants to.

THE TRUTH, THE WHOLE TRUTH, AND NOTHING BUT THE TRUTH

In an American courtroom, it is usually the bailiff who takes the oath of every witness to tell the truth, the whole truth, and nothing but the truth. If you're like me, you'll probably get the feeling that the bailiff, the witness, and, sometimes even the judge, are barely taking this truth-telling pledge seriously. Several years ago, I had the misfortune of attending a night court session in Queens, New York (as an observer only). When a witness or the accused raised his or her right hand, to me it was perfunctory and routine. Nothing more, nothing less.

One of the more interesting findings from my research, and particularly that conducted at West Point, is the emphasis on the middle part of the traditional oath—the part about the whole truth. Again, it appears that young men and women at West Point, and others leading from the high ground, go *All In!* when it comes to the truth. To them, there is no such thing as a half-truth or telling 70, 80, or 90 percent of the truth. In the minds of honorable leaders, there is only one way to approach the truth and that is by *Going All In!*

> *Honorable leaders approach the truth in the same way, by Going All In!*

In one very emotional and humbling interview, I learned how seriously West Point takes "the whole truth."

It was my fourth time up at West Point over an 18-month period. On this morning, I was scheduled to talk with an officer many years my senior.

I began the interview with what I thought was an innocuous question, "Have you had any experience with the Honor Code during your tenure here at West Point?"

There was a moment of silence when he clasped his hands together and looked upward. He didn't answer immediately.

I prompted, "Sir, would you like me to repeat the question?"

"No, that's Okay," the officer said. "I'll give you an example. A personal example ... My own son." He continued:

> He was a cadet not too long ago and he skipped post one night. He came back after he was supposed to and he was approached by a senior non-commissioned officer [NCO] who got all over him. He started asking him questions, "Where were you and what were you doing?" And my son was answering him saying that he was off post. And then he asked my son what he was doing after hours. My son answered, but he didn't answer completely and then the NCO left the room. My son never completely answered the question. He answered it in a vague way. He wasn't completely upfront with all the information that he should be upfront with. So, the NCO left the room thinking the question was answered. But, the problem was, he didn't have all the facts, because my son did not answer him totally, completely.

"Please go on," I said.

"My son left some facts out. We call this quibbling, not telling the *whole* truth. He got found for committing an honor violation and he resigned. Quibbling is very serious here. It is the lack of full disclosure. It is where you only partially answer the question."

Mark Twain once said, "The unspoken word is capital. We can invest it or we can squander it." My research tends to indicate that honorable leaders under certain circumstances may disagree with Mark Twain when they decide to *Go All In!* Leaders from the high ground usually refuse to leave facts or details hidden from view. To them, an unspoken word can never be viewed as capital when it keeps the full truth from being known. When a leader deliberately leaves out facts, the "whole" truth cannot be reached. Again, there is only one way to arrive at the "whole" truth and that is by *Going All In!*

Barely 3 weeks after this interview, I took a break from my research. With my family, I visited one of the most famous buildings on the West Point grounds. This famed building, the Cadet Chapel, is a testament to early American architecture and rivals the very best that Europe can offer in Gothic architecture. On this day, however, it wasn't the largest pipe organ in the hemisphere or the beautiful stained glass donated by previous West Point classes dating back almost a century that caught my eye. Rather, it was what my oldest daughter, Madison, brought over to me.

"Dadda, what's this mean?"

I was looking down at a small piece of paper. At the top it said "The Cadet Prayer." In particular, it was the second verse of this general and non-denominational prayer that caught my attention. It reads, "Encourage us in our endeavor to live above the common level of life. Make us to choose the harder right instead of the easier wrong, and never to be content with a half-truth when the whole can be won."

Notice the last portion of the last line—"never to be content with a half-truth when the whole can be won."

Madison was on a *Nancy Drew*–reading marathon that summer and some of it must have rubbed off on me. After the emotional interview with this very senior officer and now seeing this small portion of the Cadet Prayer, I decided to do some sleuthing of my own. Of course, in my case, there was no crime to be solved. I sought an answer to the question, "Why do honorable leaders, in general, and West Point, in particular, place such an overriding emphasis on this idea of the whole truth when many others simply dismiss or ignore it?" I was trying to understand why honorable leaders made a point of going *All In!* when it came to the truth.

The evidence is clear: Honorable leaders share a conviction that a half-truth can be more damaging than an outright lie. Stop and think about it for a minute. What kind of meal can a chef prepare with only half the recipe? What would the quality and design of a house look like if the builder or contractor had only half the plans? Could a mathematician or engineer solve complex problems if only half their theorems were true and accurate? These questions capture the danger of half-truths: Any action or process based on only partially truthful information is destined to fail. Consider the word "truthful": truth full.

Return to the "Three Rules of Thumb." Remember, the Three Rules of Thumb ask:

Rule One: Does this action attempt to deceive anyone or allow anyone to be deceived?

Rule Two: Does this action gain or allow the gain of privilege or advantage to which I or someone else would not otherwise be entitled?

Rule Three: Would I be satisfied by the outcome if I were on the receiving end of this action?

Run a half-truth through the Three Rules of Thumb. In every case, just like an outright lie, a half-truth fails the test. One defining characteristic of honorable leaders is that they do not tell half-truths when they have the whole truth at hand. In fact, the only reason to tell a half-truth is to deceive and to get something that wouldn't otherwise be available or to avoid a consequence that may be unpleasant.

That is not to say that half-truths are not popular, because they are. You may be asking why somebody would tell a half-truth rather than an outright lie. What advantage does one think he is gaining by using a half-truth instead of a lie? The answer requires a return to the R-word.

Remember that a core component of rationalization, the R-word, is to deflect responsibility from oneself. The R-word manufactures a justification or an excuse where none should exist. This interaction between the R-word and half-truths makes a dangerous combination.

Perhaps the best way to see how this plays out is to return to the initial case involving the son of the senior officer. In this young man's honor hearing, he claimed that he didn't lie and that he had told a majority of the truth. When a low elevation leader is searching for a rationalization, this is among the best—"I didn't out and out lie and most of what I told was the truth." Low elevation leaders engaging in half-truths convince themselves that they're not doing anything wrong because they aren't totally lying and are, they reason, telling a portion of the truth. The Three Rules of Thumb perform as designed and we know that half-truths fulfill the same function as lies and do so in a manner that is harder to detect, making them all the more dangerous.

Those who lead from the high ground recognize that half-truths are not good enough and that reliance on half-truths will keep a leader in the valley on the low ground. My interviews with men and women who "stand their ground" indicate that they understand that what we don't say is often as important as what we do say. Silence when the full truth is known is a convenient way to hide information that could influence an outcome. In the case of the young man who quibbled to his NCO, the cadet knew that his punishment would be worse if he disclosed that he was drinking underage off post. Realizing that, he left this information out.

> *Half-truths are almost always more dangerous than full-blown lies.*

Suppose there were a 7-day delay before you could read your e-mails. Or consider a patient who must make a decision for life or death surgery based on a single laboratory test. What might happen to the NASA space shuttle if key decision-makers only received the positive, never the negative, information? After the shuttle *Columbia* incinerated when returning to Earth in February 2003, the *Columbia* Accident Investigation Board concluded that this was precisely what doomed *Columbia*'s crew of seven to fiery death. One surefire way to assure disaster is to make decisions and act on the basis of only half the relevant information. Indeed, sometimes leaders will have to make decisions based on limited information. But a leader should never have to jeopardize a project, the finances of others, or the lives of others, with limited information when all the information is readily available.

> *What we don't say is sometimes more important than what we do say.*

Not only is complete and timely communication important to the leader, it is essential to the functioning of any organization. Full disclosure is the grease that enables organizations to function. Before decisions can be made and people can act, there is always communication. An organization that communicates by half-truths is severely handicapped and, in all likelihood, is destined for failure. Leaders on the high ground are intimately aware of this necessity and are never satisfied with a half-truth. Instead, they choose to *Go All In!* to secure the whole truth.

THE END GAME

Meet John Amore. In late spring or early summer, 2002, Mr. Amore gathered prospective Wall Street traders to let them in on his special plan. Although the stock market was in a precipitous decline during this period, he detailed a surefire way for traders to make money at his firm of A.B. Watley.

Mr. Amore and his band of traders relied heavily on branch office brokers at the world's top firms, such as Merrill Lynch. The branch office brokers would allegedly leave their phones off the hook to allow Mr. Amore and others to listen in on in-house stock transactions piped over a variant of speakerphone known as a squawk box. Brokers at Mr. Amore's firm would take this information from eavesdropping and would immediately buy or sell just before the big boys. Thus, A.B. Watley was able to profit by grabbing the optimum stock price before large institutional investors could fill their orders. Consequently, these institutions would buy shares for more or sell them for less, with the impact usually trickling down to mutual fund investors, pension fund beneficiaries, and others whose savings are guarded by Wall Street's biggest players. Reporters Aaron Lucchetti and Kara Scannell from the *Wall Street Journal* demonstrated how this played out:

- Around 12:04 p.m. on Feb 5, 2003. A Merrill Lynch trader issues a call over the squawk box to purchase a big block of American Financial Group stock shares.
- A Merrill Lynch broker allows traders from A.B. Watley to listen in on an upcoming transaction. Brokers at A.B. Watley immediately buy 10,000 shares of American Financial Group at $19.79.
- Somewhere between 12:08 and 12:38, Merrill Lynch purchases a large volume of American Financial stock. As a result, the stock price rises slightly.
- A.B. Whatley unloads its 10,000 shares at or around 12:51 for $19.99, making a gross profit of more than $2,000—in less than 50 minutes.

SEC investigators say the Amore-led group of A.B. Whatley amassed more than $650,000 in profits from hundreds of such transactions in 2002 and 2003. Despite this rather attractive outcome, it is clear that traders at A.B. Whatley and several brokers from mainstream institutional investors achieved this outcome in the wrong way. Their circumvention of SEC trading rules and regulations, and the offering and acceptance of privileged and "insider" information resulted in several fines and criminal indictments. [5]

Would honorable leaders endorse such a practice? Would West Point support such a scheme? No. At West Point, it is possible to score more points than an opponent during an intramural athletic event and still lose the game. How can that be? Referees and officers can disqualify a winning team for demonstrating poor sportsmanship.

It is hard to look at these two cases and not marvel at the differences. In the first case, the leader of A.B. Watley, Mr. Amore, valued winning the financial game more than playing by the rules. A belief shared by West Point men and women and by honorable leaders elsewhere is that, while winning is important, *how* a person, team, or organization wins is equally important. Some scholars refer to this as a means-versus-end argument. I refer to it as the process-outcome (PO) model. In terms of honorable leadership, to secure the high ground, equal due must be given to both process and outcome. One can't be sacrificed or ignored for the other. Honorable leaders *Go All In!* by holding true to both the outcomes and processes associated with winning. Those who lead from the high ground can do both—secure favorable outcomes (O) and demand legitimate processes (P).

If someone believes that West Point is not a competitive place or that West Point puts less value on outcomes than other organizations, my response will be—think again. Few organizations sustain the performance-oriented atmosphere of West Point where every aspect of a young man or woman's life is carefully evaluated. From room appearance to wearing the uniform to the number of push-ups to performance in the classroom to evaluations by peers and subordinates, West Point's existence is rooted in the premise Never Lose. When it comes to our nation's defense, failure is not an option. In spite of this standard to perform under the severest pressure, winning at all costs while dismissing the process (P) is forbidden at West Point and by others who lead from the high ground. *Going All In!* and securing the high ground need both the O and the P.

LOOKING GOOD?

In the course of my research, a colleague and close friend of mine, Tom Hawk, gave me some material to look over. Tom Hawk, a graduate of the United States Naval Academy (USNA), shared with me an ethics book that his class of 1964 gave to the graduating class of 2004. Although the book is filled with several meaningful mini cases, the one I enjoyed the most is relevant to this particular point and is simply titled, "Canteen Tops."[6] Because it's such an important case, I've taken the liberty of reproducing much of it below:

> A new commanding general (CG) was going to conduct a personal inspection of every unit, down to companies within battalions in his division. One item he focused on was the lowly canteen cap. Even though it costs only a few cents, it's vital to the Marine in the field who survives on water. A canteen without a top will lose water as the Marine conducts field operations.
>
> During an inspection of one company, the CG asked the company commander about canteen tops. The company commander was able to answer truthfully that he had all the canteen tops he was supposed to have.
>
> During his regular inspections, the CG had been asking company commanders, platoon leaders, and individual Marines about the status of canteen tops. The CG had learned that tops were scarce because the contracts for ordering them weren't a high priority among professional supply officers who were more concerned with getting the big-ticket necessities. However, to a Marine in the field, a canteen top was a necessity. The system wasn't as responsive as it should have been.
>
> Because he knew his company was due for inspection by the CG, the company commander in this case went to his peers in other units and persuaded them to lend him some canteens and tops for the inspection. He promised to return them later.
>
> On the day of the inspection, the company commander was ready. Each Marine in his company had a canteen with a top.

In this case, the company commander led from a valley, not the high ground, and the general sensed it. The CG asked the company commander if he had borrowed the canteens for the purpose of looking good during the inspection. The company commander admitted that he had. There is something profoundly intuitive in the general's response.

> When I'm inspecting, I'm not just looking at an individual unit. I'm inspecting the entire division. If you willfully cover up how inept the supply system is, you're not demonstrating loyalty. In fact, your cover-up is worse than just a simple lack of canteen tops. I know the problems in the supply system. I realize that not having canteen tops is not a reflection on you or your unit. However, your attempt to grandstand and look good is a problem. You could have contributed, either knowingly or unknowingly, to my making a bad decision based on faulty information that you gave me. You may have a great future in front of you. But I don't think it's in the Marine Crops.

The moment a leader places achieving outcomes (O) and looking good above following processes (P), something dangerous begins to occur to the Ps. Clearly, when a leader values Os more than Ps, Ps can get ignored. When this occurs, many important organizational Ps and systems never get tested or, if they do get tested, are hardly stressed to their full capacity. When Ps and other systems are not put under stress or forced to perform, they tend to erode. This erosion of Ps often worsens since low elevation leaders become less reliant on Ps and organizational systems to assure their Os. People begin to create their own Ps and systems to get their Os. In classic low-ground style, we saw how the unit commander didn't rely on or test the supply system to get the canteen caps. Instead, he brokered personal deals and borrowed to temporarily get his canteen caps. The problem is that organizations need consistent and stable Ps and systems to continue to function. This cannot occur when leaders devise their own unique way of circumventing an inadequate system. Organizational chaos can occur when the proper system is ignored or broken and is replaced by hundreds of makeshift remedies to solve the same problem. In the case of the canteen tops, it is easy to imagine a crisis when the Marines desperately needed canteen tops. Because outcomes (O) were allowed to trump processes (P), the supply system could cave or might not be able to respond to the surge in demand.

One colonel with whom I spent some time told me of this case within his unit. A warrant officer was signing off on all maintenance checks without actually performing the maintenance, a practice commonly referred to as "pencil whipping." The perceived need for efficiency motivated this warrant officer to pencil whip. It took him seconds to sign off on the paperwork, but many minutes to actually perform the maintenance check. He believed that he didn't have the time. He also wanted to look good. He didn't want others to suspect that there could be any problem with his helicopter. This kind of maintenance masked some serious problems with the performance of that helicopter—problems that were discovered only after it crashed. If the warrant officer had led from the high ground, process (P) and outcome (O) would have received equal attention and the crash would have not occurred.

> *Ps won't be there when a leader or organization needs them most if they've never been put to the test.*

After I had conducted all the interviews and had collected data from far and near, what I didn't hear and didn't see distinguished the honorable leaders who *Go All In!* from others. Not once did I hear an honorable leader say to his or her employees, "Just get it done! I don't care how you do it." That would send the signal that it's okay to ignore the P to get to the desired O. Honorable leaders wouldn't do that. Not once did I see or hear an honorable leader turn a blind eye to Os gained by manipulating or ignoring the Ps. Just the opposite. Honorable leaders did what the commanding general did to the unit commander borrowing canteen lids: made it clear to all that Ps were as important as Os.

Let me finish by noting that my research overwhelmingly indicates that honorable leaders *Go All In!* by seeing Process and Outcome theories as one and the same. It may be easy to focus on one element at the expense of the other, but *Going All In!* means doing both. It is the capacity to win, but only by doing so the *right* way.

FIRESTARTER

In the course of preparing for this book, I decided to conduct an experiment, not a scientific experiment with independent, dependent, and control variables. No, this was more of a quick field experiment.

I asked one of my teaching assistants to randomly choose 30 dates over a six-month period. After she selected those dates, I instructed her to get the *Wall Street Journal* for every date that she chose. She was then to check the first five pages of the *Wall Street Journal* for any cases of fraud, theft, corruption, or scandal. She was to give me the number of honor breaches found during her random selection of these 30 dates. Repeat stories were not to count.

She came back about a week later with a surprising number—47.

"You must be mistaken, I asked you to only select thirty dates."

"That's what I did."

"What?" I asked.

"Yeah. On every one of those days there was something bad going on."

I still didn't get it, "That still only equals thirty, not forty-seven."

"No, most times there were at least two bad articles within the first five pages!"

One takeaway from this quick field experiment is that it validates what we know to be true—there is a lack of honorable leadership out there.

There was much more, though, behind this little trial. I stayed up that evening and personally reviewed the 47 articles and, in every case, the people involved were reasonably to exceptionally educated, moderately to extremely wealthy, and held substantial leadership positions within their organization or company. I couldn't help but think that many of these organizations had invested in leadership development either by retaining consultants or by in-house training. No doubt, the names of the training would vary, like character building, integrity enhancement, or some other momentary buzzword. These organizations had to invest in such development, didn't they? I took my hunch to several high-level managers. All responded that they did receive some type of leadership or character training. The research questions to me became, "Given all this training, why did it never catch fire? Why didn't the message stick? Why didn't it spread?"

The answers to these questions lie in this *All In!* concept, but in ways markedly different than discussed so far. The reason that honorable leaders are who they are and that honorable groups, teams, and organizations are who they are is they take an *All In!* approach to integrating the principles of honorable leadership. What this means is that a one-day seminar on honorable leadership is not going to result in much. Emphasizing honorable leadership in one part of an organization such as human resources, but ignoring it in others such as finance, accounting, operations, or sales, will not result in much. Purely academic programs to develop honorable leaders without allowing individuals to practice what they have learned will not result in much. None of these methods are *All In!* commitments. They are merely incremental, isolated, limited, and handicapped tactics. They will fail.

To really reach the high ground, the fundamentals of honorable leadership need to be fully integrated into every facet of an organization. It needs to be pervasive and embedded in the fabric or culture of a team, group, or organization. The values and norms of honorable leadership must be given priority.

Reading media accounts and visiting, for-profit and non-profit, corporate websites reveals no commitment to integration. Instead, it seems that most organizations are taking a segmented and parochial approach to honor, character, ethics, and integrity. Take, for instance, the fad of creating a chief ethics officer. On the surface, this may seem like a good idea. But taking a high-ground perspective, I suspect that honorable leaders would reject this practice. I can anticipate the criticism from those perched on the high ground: "Shouldn't everyone be an ethics officer?" Or, "Why does only one person have the sole responsibility for promoting and protecting honor? Isn't that the duty of all?"

West Point law professor Kevin Govern remarked, "[Ethics integration] is something that has to be done *every day in every way*." Lieutenant Colonel Govern makes an effort to devote a couple of minutes every day in his law classes to the subject of values or "something that deals with ethics." He's not teaching a military ethics class, nor is it a philosophy class. But he makes an effort to *integrate* the principles of honorable leadership into his law curriculum.

One cadet with whom I spoke said,

> The Superintendent [equivalent to a university president] and the Commandant [equivalent to a university provost] are the biggest cheerleaders for the honor and respect training that goes on at West Point. If the Superintendent is willing to put that much time into honor training, then just maybe it's important. And I think it really does have to come form the top. Yes, you need to grow that culture from the bottom, but if you don't have the top's overwhelming support, then there's no point because if the institution's not supporting it, then what am I, the one guy, going to do?

Some may dismiss this message from this 21-year-old young man. Examined closely, his statement reflects a radical departure from the status quo. West Point cadets own and administer the Honor Code and that is important. But, in itself, this isn't enough. Upper leadership needs to commit to *Go All In!* When these conditions are met, the entire organization is canvassed. The top is pushing their priority of honorable leadership *down*, while the bottom is pushing that same priority *up*.

The way to think about the ignition and spread of honorable leadership is to compare it to a natural-occurring phenomenon, fire. Fire is pretty straightforward. To start one, you must have three things: oxygen, heat, and fuel.

Wind (that has oxygen) helps with spreading a fire. With only one variable missing, fires won't start. The same can be said for the spread of honorable leadership. A piecemeal approach will never work. Instead, all ingredients must be present. Once all ingredients are identified, they must be put *All In!*

Are You In or Are You Out?

The dealer is waiting. Are you going to fold? Or do you want to *Go All In!* Nobody will blame you if you put your cards down and walk away. *Going All In!* requires a 100 percent commitment of time, a 100 percent commitment to the whole truth, and a 100 percent commitment to both processes and outcomes. It is damned tough to *Go All In!* Few have the guts to do it. But, thankfully, this isn't poker and it may be less of a gamble than you think. There's no need to play the hand by yourself. You are not alone.

6

Who's Got Your Back?

E Pluribus Unum—Out of Many, One
—Taken from the Great Seal of the United States
on the U.S. Dollar Bill

Norman R. Augustine was the former Chairman and CEO of Martin Marietta Corporation. By all accounts, Norman R. Augustine is an honorable leader. His many accomplishments include the National Medal of Technology given by the president of the United States and the NASA Distinguished Public Service Award. In 1999, he received West Point's highest honor, the Sylvanus Thayer Award for exemplifying the ideals of West Point reflected in its motto, "Duty, Honor, Country." On April 3, 1992, KSJN National Public Radio decided to carry Mr. Augustine's speech that he gave to the leaders of Martin Marietta at their Minnesota meeting. It was during this speech that Mr. Augustine made a particularly interesting point when he emphasized, "Ethics is a highly personal matter."[1]

Many argue that A.J. Kitt has done more for U.S. downhill skiing than any single individual. As the only U.S. man ever to race in four Olympics, he is largely credited for resurrecting competitive skiing in the United States. Now a spokesperson for Rolex and also a credentialed motivational speaker, A.J. Kitt is noted for remarking, "You have no control over what the other guy does. You only have control over what you do."

You might be wondering why these two individuals and why these particular quotes. I chose these quotes because many managers, including the very best and brightest, tend to buy-in to these messages. Majority status aside, however, my research, the research of others, and the very lives of those who spoke those words suggest something completely different.

WHEN *BE* BECOMES *WE*

Let's examine these quotes. First, we have Mr. Augustine's notion that *ethics* is an individual choice. No doubt, the ultimate ethical decision rests with the individual. But, return to the idea of *moments* and intersections. Are we truly ever alone? How many long road trips do we go on by ourselves? Probably, not many. Even on small commutes these days, the radio is playing. There's music, and, maybe some advertisements. Or, for the sake of argument, let's say the radio is off. In that case, we're likely talking on a cell phone. The point here is that we're really not alone and our decisions aren't always completely ours to make. We may think they are, but, in reality, we are almost always under some influence. This is the problem with these quotes. In essence, the remarks by Mr. Augustine and A.J. Kitt assume that decisions are made singly and are immune to any influence. This is by no means an attack on Mr. Augustine or A.J. Kitt. In fact, it's just the opposite. Undeniably, both have positively influenced thousands of Americans to *do* better and *be* better. And it is for precisely that reason that I respectfully disagree with their quotes. Both of them, either through mentoring, role modeling, or just through the relationships that they've had with others, demonstrate how much influence and impact one person can have on another. Because of honorable leaders like them, rest assured that we are not alone. As we speed through *moments* and intersections, adjust your rear view mirror and look in the backseat. Chances are there's somebody back there you recognize.

> *One of the most effective ways to improve upon the* BE *is to build a strong* WE.

An important caveat to this discussion and where these quotes can inform us is drawing our attention back to the BE. If a leader cannot BE right, then it is difficult to Do right. Indeed, the notion of the individual, of the BE is critical to our discussion. Considering all possible factors, however, it appears that the greatest way to improve upon the BE is to build a strong WE.

A GOOD *WE* TRUMPS A GREAT *BE*

Don't say WE doesn't matter to the likes of Roy Mullet, Cheryl Denise Thomas, Frank Mistretta, Bobby Newman, or Steven Battaglia. All of them relied on each other, on friends, or on family to survive the 2005 devastation of Hurricane Katrina in New Orleans.[2] As Bobby Newman would later put it, "The only way we'd make it was if we stayed together." Not a single one of them found a rooftop, a piece of dry high ground, or a treetop without the help of another. Despite the Mississippi River rising 11 feet in several hours and 20-foot surge waves occurring in their literal back yard, those who stuck together improved their chances of beating one of the worst natural disasters ever to hit U.S. soil.

In most cases, the only way to *Secure the High Ground* is to rely on the assistance of another. Leaders don't have to climb to the summit by themselves, and often they can't do it by themselves.

> *There is NO good reason why a leader should ever climb alone.*

More often than not, there are helpers or guides. Few, if any, journeys to the high ground are solo ones. Rather, they tend to be social. To be sure, all great military battles for the high ground from Cemetery Ridge at Gettysburg to Iwo Jima required the will of the many, not the few.

Are You Good Enough?

When I look over the paths and stories of honorable leaders, they all seem to realize early that while a strong BE is good, it is rarely good enough. Wagering it all on the BE is just plain naïve. Every human, every leader, is prone to falter. A common belief shared by honorable leaders, which distinguished them from everybody else, is their awareness that they could never reach the high ground without the help of other great people.

My discussion with Bryan Herrin, a 21-year-old West Point junior from Austin, Texas makes this point.

> It's an honor violation to sign out somewhere and not go there or, even worse, blow post [leave West Point and the Hudson Valley area]. One way that this could be done is to sign out on Walking Privileges down to Highland Falls, knowing all along you're not going there, but go to New York City instead. Well, I had a friend who was going to pick up his girlfriend in Newburgh at the airport there and it was during the academic year and during the week, so he didn't have the privileges to do that, and he was talking about how he would sign out on walking privileges down to Highland Falls, but instead go to the airport. And we listened to his idea and we were like "Listen to what you're saying. If you do that, you're compromising your honor. Just take a moment and think about this. There are other ways to do this." And he was like, "You're right. I need to think about what I'm doing here."

He paused. "At West Point," Bryan continued, "we play on this like Watch Your Buddy. By doing that, we can preempt somebody from compromising his honor."

This anecdote brings me to a major point of honorable leaders and honorable organizations. Most, if not all, strive to get a backseat driver *before* they approach a *moment* or intersection. Think for a moment what a backseat driver does. A backseat driver cares about the details of making the trip. Many of the best "worst backseat drivers" are constantly aware and offering opinions. They may annoy, but backseat drivers are really there to make you more aware, to protect. How difficult is it to read a map while barreling down the highway at 65 mph? Wouldn't another passenger—a "copilot"—make it so much easier? And deep down, we know they're doing it not to aggravate, but because they care. When this young man brought this honor issue to Bryan and his friends, what he really was saying was, "Help me, here. I'm approaching a *moment*. I'm not equipped. I'm going too fast. Help me drive." Even though he probably didn't *want* to hear that he would not be able to pick up his girlfriend and that he would have to pay the $100 for a taxi, he knew that he *needed* to hear it. This subtle difference between *want* and *need* is magnified when one is around honorable leaders.

Continuing with this analogy, honorable leaders don't fight the traffic in Baltimore, Washington, D.C., or Pittsburgh alone. Instead, they want someone there to assist as copilot on the passenger side or from the backseat. It is tough to face *moments* or highway intersections like those found in places like D.C., so honorable leaders are never too proud to ask for help. They say "I don't know how to get there" or "I'm not comfortable, will you go with me?" It often requires more courage to ask for help when approaching a *moment* than to drive solo. An important point here is that not only do honorable leaders know their own boundaries, their own limitations, they are also willing to share them with others by seeking help. In addition to courage, humility is also needed here.

Another reason why someone should be sitting shotgun or in the backseat is that, at one time or another, we all get lazy, drowsy, and, even, downright sleepy. One of the great movie scenes occurs in the 1983 classic *National Lampoon's Vacation.* Committed to having a "fun" family trip, Clark Griswold takes his family on a cross-country drive in search of Wally World. In one of their more serious missteps along the way, Clark falls asleep at the wheel driving just outside St. Louis. In the process, he ends up tearing through several yards, crosses several lanes of congested traffic, and barely misses a man walking his poodle before settling his wagon into a hotel parking lot. Jokes aside, drowsy driving and falling asleep at the wheel is a serious problem. In fact, the National Highway Traffic Safety Administration (NHSTA) estimates that at least 100,000 police-reported crashes are the direct result of fatigue. The price tag for fatigue is also quite steep: 1,500 deaths, 71,000 injuries, and $12.5 billion in monetary losses.[3] It is the inability of the sleeping driver to be aware (see Chapter 2) that makes this type of accident particularly severe. Of course, one of the most effective ways to prevent this is to pack your vehicle with people dedicated to your safety,

> *Get another passenger or a backseat driver when you feel yourself getting weak or tired.*

their safety. When this occurs, drowsily speeding through dangerous *moments* or intersections is much less likely to occur because other people are keeping you focused, alert. Imagine for one second what would've been the outcome if Bryan's friend had not asked for help from one of his backseat drivers. There is little doubt that a crash would ensue.

Closely related to this idea is that as a leader's confidence grows, helpers will not always be necessary. In the scenario with Bryan's friend, after sharing his concerns and listening to what trusted others had to say, there is a greater likelihood that he could do it himself the next time he comes across a similar *moment* or intersection. This is real-world proof that the BE gets stronger through the WE. Reflect on your own situation. How often do you need somebody to accompany you to a new or busy place? For me, it is usually only once. After going to Heinz Field in Pittsburgh with a friend, I knew where the routes, the potholes, and the dangerous intersections were. The next time, I felt more comfortable going by myself. The story of Bryan Herrin's classmate reflects a pattern common to almost all honorable leaders: They build their BE by relying on a strong WE.

Unless automotive technology changes drastically between the writing of this sentence and the publishing of this book, there will still be one steering wheel, one clutch, one accelerator pedal, and one brake pedal inside every car. It is necessary to raise this point to illustrate that the controls and the ultimate decision to turn left, right, or brake still rests with one person, the driver. Passengers can help, but the decision is ultimately the driver's, or the honorable leader's. Honorable leaders make a big deal about this. They seek the guidance and wisdom of others. But they understand that the right choice in a *moment*

> *The WE can support the BE, but it can never replace the BE. The ultimate decision will always rest with the BE, the individual.*

remains the ultimate responsibility of the BE, not the WE. In the case of Bryan's friend, he found wise guidance from the WE. His WE did their job. They made him more aware, more focused. But the decision to embrace or ignore the WE was his to make. His trusted WE prevented a head-on collision with West Point's Honor Code. He listened to his friends and preserved his honor.

Norm

Remember James Kehoe who was the West Point cadet Honor Captain when I interviewed him in 2004? He managed the cadet side of the academy's honor system. My question to him was simple, "How do you do it? If honor can be taught as you propose, what is the greatest tool for accomplishing this?"

This young man of 21 or 22 studied me closely. I got the feeling that he was impatient that I didn't understand such a basic and core concept. He responded,

The one thing that I would say is, we change what the norm is. If the norm in high school is to be able to cheat, well, the minute you come here, you realize that is not the norm anymore. And maybe it's human nature to want to be like the norm, so if you set up West Point to where the norm is always to be truthful, always be honest, now people will abide by that and you start to believe in what you're doing.

To more fully appreciate James's comments, some insight into the causes and drivers of human behavior is needed. The nature–nurture controversy is the launching point for such discussions. At one end, many believe that genetics, heredity affect human decisions and behaviors. A great example of this is personality, which leading researchers conclude is heavily determined by genetic make-up. Some people are just naturally more agreeable, more sociable, or more creative than others. As strong as a person's personality is, however, most behavioral psychologists and experts in organizational behavior believe that the situations or the environment where we find ourselves impacts individual choice and behavior more. A few researchers have further discriminated between strong situations and strong cultures versus weak ones. For instance, Marine Boot Camp at Paris Island fits the definition of a strong situation, strong culture. Regardless of personality type, new recruits tend to act similarly, even in unison—despite varied and distinct personalities and upbringings. This phenomenon is easily explained by situational and environmental factors. The phenomenon is best explained by what James Kehoe astutely understood—the presence of norms.

Norms are the rules and patterns of behavior that are accepted, expected, and encouraged by members of a group, team, or organization. It should be of little surprise that every team, group, or organization establishes or enforces some set of norms. Without norms, people don't act in concert, they act solely as individuals. Without norms, there would be chaos. Norms are even more important because they define the behaviors that members of a group or organization believe to be necessary, essential, to meet its mission and goals. Norms serve as unwritten rules and unspoken cues that shape human decisions and behaviors. Another way to view norms is as a type of social glue that keeps people acting together to accomplish a certain task. Norms are exceptionally interesting because they are difficult to draw, measure, or touch. They exist, but only in the abstract. And for these reasons, to harbor control over the construction, development, and deployment of such norms is a skill that sets people apart in both good and not-so-good ways.

> *Norms are among the most reliable predictors of human behavior.*

Who Do Ya Know?

Consider the following cases. Prosecutors in Singapore in 2005 brought the curtain down on China Aviation Oil, a large jet-fuel trading firm. At least five senior executives and directors were charged with crimes including forgery, insider trading, and publishing false financial statements. Chen Jiulin, the suspended CEO, was charged with fifteen offenses and the Chairman of the Board, Jia Changbin, was accused of insider trading.[4]

Mull over what happened at Boston Scientific. Boston Scientific agreed to a $74 million settlement for an incomplete recall of one of its cardiac stent systems. Stents are used to open clogged arteries and they generate about $5.5 billion in global annual sales. Unfortunately for Boston Scientific, their Nir-Sox stents didn't inflate properly. This malfunction caused at least 26 injuries according to the U.S. Food and Drug Administration. The government said that Boston Scientific's management "unanimously decided" on September 16, 1998, that the device should be pulled from the market. But, on that same day, they authorized the shipment of 840 units. Senior management knew there was a serious problem in the functioning of the stent, but decided to market it anyway.[5]

It was a family affair for the Adelphia Cable scandal where shareholder dollars were spent for personal use. John Rigas and his son, Tim Rigas, received jail terms in 2005 for engaging in such fraud.[6]

Or contemplate the case at WorldCom. It just wasn't Bernard Ebbers. There was Betty Vinson, the former WorldCom accounting manager, who pled guilty for her role in the WorldCom collapse. There was Troy Normand, another accounting manager, who also pled guilty. Don't forget Buford Yates, the director of general accounting, or David Myers, the former WorldCom controller, both of whom pled guilty to wrongdoing in the demise of WorldCom.[7]

Then there is *Mara Salvatrucha*. Commonly referred to as just MS-13, *Mara Salavatrucha* is one of the fastest growing gangs in the United States. The gang attracted people fleeing El Salvador during times of civil war, many of whom were guerilla fighters. The gang has taken root in such places as Washington, D.C., and has gained notoriety for being particularly cohesive and violent. A January 2005 machete attack on a teenage boy in Alexandria, VA, and the July 2003 slaying of a pregnant 17-year-old, MS-13 former member turned government informant raised the profile of this tight and "hard-to-crack" gang.[8]

Majors Nate Allen and Tony Burgess go back a long way. Friends from West Point, they became even closer when they commanded army companies at about the same time in Hawaii. Company command in the U.S. Army is one of the most rewarding, demanding, and difficult assignments during a typical, 20-year army career. As company commanders, Allen and Burgess shared a sense of isolation when they encountered a problem or developed a solution. They had no effective way of sharing their concerns or resolutions. In the army of the 1990s, when a new idea was generated it had to go high up the bureaucracy and through several levels of validation before it could be published. Certainly, this approach was slow and ineffective. With the help of a couple other majors and captains, Allen and Burgess pooled funds and devoted countless hours to start Companycommand.com and Platoonleader.org. What these Internet websites did was to allow a company commander in Korea to either share or request information on an issue for which a commander in, say Italy, may already have the answer. All in real time. The real value of these websites is that they provide a global and quick way to share important solutions to common challenges faced by many junior leaders in the army. The fascinating point of this story is that this small group of four or five officers decided to donate this intellectual property to the U.S. Army. West Point's former Academic Dean, Brigadier General Daniel Kaufman, valued the intellectual capital of these websites at over $50 million. Currently, these websites have proved invaluable during conflicts in Iraq and Afghanistan as junior leaders can now share life-saving lessons throughout the army community across the globe in seconds. The army learns lessons faster and better because of these websites.

If you take these scenarios together—the creation of the army websites and the other cases—you reach quite a radical conclusion about norms. Norms can lead to the high ground or they can lead down to the swamps. In the first several cases, every instance of corruption involved more than one person. Just as building honor is a social practice, dishonor or corruption is also a social enterprise. We can see in the case of MS-13 how they relied and built their organization around norms, which were leveraged to achieve deadly outcomes. The fulcrum here is the leadership portion of the *honorable leadership* quotient. Honorable leaders build and influence norms to produce positive ethical outcomes that meet the honorable goals of the organization.

For all of their strengths, norms are really at the mercy of leadership. Leaders can use norms to go up as in the case of Allen and Burgess or leaders can use norms to go down as in the cases of WorldCom or MS-13. Invariably, those that lead from the high ground knowingly and carefully use norms to achieve greatness, never to cause despair or harm to others.

> *How leaders build and utilize norms determines whether the leader and group are going UP or DOWN in elevation.*

ACCOUNTS PAYABLE

Switch gears for a second and think about the most effective way to stick to a diet. Or better yet, type in "diet" at Google. To read media accounts and websites, there are really only two ways to stick to a diet. One is through individual willpower. One of the more intriguing websites relies on this approach and even suggests that we brainwash ourselves. You may wonder how you go about doing that. Their recommendation is straightforward, but scary. Just speak to yourself every day 400 to 500 times with affirmations such as, "I can do this." I don't know about you, but I'm not sure that I can repeat to myself, out loud, the same message 400 to 500 times a day. Not only annoying, this tactic is inefficient. Relying solely on independent will or on the BE is a losing proposition. There must be more.

The other approach is to go with medication or elective surgery. Both carry risks. With medication, there is the risk of addiction or dependence. Also, when the drugs go away, so may the diet. Surgery such as "stomach stapling" is becoming more popular. But it carries a risk of rebound in that the patient's obesity may return worse than before surgery if post-surgical follow-up stops.

Maybe the best place to look for answers is to carefully examine what most people credit as the most successful dieting program ever—the Atkins Diet. The truth about the diet is that there is conflicting research on how well it works or if it even works at all. Some experts link the diet to increased risks of osteoporosis, heart disease, colon cancer, and renal disease. The diet is high in saturated fats and cholesterol, and low on fiber.

I was eating dinner with some close friends in Blacksburg, Virginia, who said they followed the Atkins Diet. Both had lost a good deal of weight so it seemed that Atkins had worked for them. But on closer investigation, maybe their weight-loss was due to something entirely different from the Atkins plan.

My friend remarked, "I just got caught up in it. I told all my friends, all my family, that I was going on this Atkins Diet."

His wife added, "Me, too! Everybody was doing Atkins at work and I got carried away and I started telling everybody that I was going on a diet."

The husband continued, "Then a remarkable thing happened. It took on a life of its own. Like a snowball. I couldn't go anywhere without a friend or someone from my family asking me how the diet was going. I had told everybody that cared about me that I was doing Atkins, and because they cared, they kept on asking me about it. It began to be annoying. But in a way, it was for this reason that I lost the 25 pounds in six months. I didn't want to answer to my friends and my family that I quit or that it just wasn't working, especially when it seemed like it worked for everybody else."

The real reason that the Atkins Diet may work, especially compared to countless other diet programs, is that this particular dieting program has taken on a social life of its own. Prior to the Atkins program, dieting was largely a personal, private thing. With Atkins, we now have a social event.

The social part is critical. It is easy to let ourselves down. Most people don't think twice about reneging on a promise they make to themselves, but wouldn't consider reneging when a friend is involved. One explanation is that we tend to accept our own R-word much better than others would. Somehow, we instinctively know that the only person who truly buys the R-word is the one in the mirror. Closely related to this point is the fact that it is much easier to break promises to ourselves than it is to break promises to others. This fact is readily apparent in my friend's words. He wasn't going to give up on his diet because too

> *While it can be quite easy to ignore promises and commitments made to ourselves, it is harder to do so when others are involved.*

many people knew and too many people were going to ask him about it. While he could accept failing himself, he didn't want to be viewed as a failure by his significant others. Peer pressure can be powerful. And peer pressure doesn't always suggest a bad thing like drug use. In fact, I found that many honorable leaders leveraged peer pressure in a positive way that made them better equipped to reach the high ground.

What does the phenomenon of a high-fat diet craze have to do with honorable leadership? Quite a bit. Honorable leaders seem to build their internal will by leveraging external ties. Evidence of this can be seen in the actions of Bryan's West Point friend. On the surface, it may seem that this young man's initial behavior was dishonorable. I don't think so. Deep down he knew that he couldn't survive this *moment* by himself, so he brought internal feelings and weaknesses out into the open. What was once internal—the thought of lying to pick up his girlfriend—became external after he raised the issue with his friends. He was asking for backseat drivers. But equally important, he was creating an "accountability network" much the way my friend did with his Atkins Diet. Great friends like Bryan were going to hold him accountable. They'd ask, "How did you decide to get your girlfriend" or "Can I help you think of another way to get your girlfriend." This young man strengthened his internal honor backbone via an external network, spotters if you will. You got the sense from Bryan's story that the young man in desperate need of his girlfriend was willing to let himself down and to compromise his own honor. But, after he shared his feelings with his friends, he was not going to let *them* down.

This dialogue reveals a humble truth about those who lead from the top: None of them is a superhero, which should give hope to all. Instead, I witnessed men and women who knew their own limitations and who were willing to invite others close to them to help them overcome their *moments* of weakness. These honorable leaders create what I term, an accounts payable network. On things that really matter, make a promise or a commitment to yourself. But to triumph over *moments* of weakness, set up an account payable with somebody else. Make a commitment or a promise to someone you respect, whom you care about. Although we may let ourselves down, we don't like to disappoint people we respect and care about.

HATE TO TOLERATE

West Point's Honor Code reads "A cadet will not lie, cheat, steal, or tolerate those who do."

Maybe the most difficult portion of the Honor Code to put into practice is the last five words—"or tolerate those who do." By West Point standards, tolerating acts of dishonor is as bad as committing the act itself. Cadets have been dismissed from the academy for witnessing acts of cheating, stealing, and lying, and choosing to remain silent. Put plainly, when a West Point man or woman observes somebody violating the Honor Code, they must tell.

They Have No Choice

This component of the Honor Code is a radical departure from how most of us were raised and socialized. We can see it on a kindergarten playground. Nobody wants to be labeled a tattletale. A couple years later, the words change, but the concept remains the same. I've repeatedly heard words like "nobody wants to rat on a classmate." Picture the connotation of rat. A rat is a sneaky, garbage-eating rodent. In the business and corporate community, we hear words like whistle-blower. The connotation, like rat, is not always favorable.

Let's do a more sophisticated analysis of the assumptions behind these negative connotations. It appears that loyalty to friends or family should supersede honor, character, and integrity. Since honorable leadership is such a social practice, it does stand to reason that social relationships can work for or against a leader.

In one of my very first interviews with a West Point graduate and now a major in the U. S. Army, I saw how much West Point struggles with this idea of non-toleration. When the issue of toleration came up, he admitted that when he was a cadet he tolerated some friends, also West Point cadets, who had lied to some officers. They were never caught and, to this day, he still questions what had happened. Dave Jones, the high-ranking officer at the Simon Center for the Professional Military Ethic, was not fazed when I brought this up to him, "It's the biggest thing cadets struggle with. We all struggle with telling on somebody else. That doesn't go away. We all have peers."

There's a lot riding on this issue of loyalty versus honor. A couple of hundred miles south of West Point in Annapolis, Maryland, is West Point's sea service counterpart, the United States Naval Academy. The Naval Academy does not have a toleration clause in its Honor Code. Knowing this, I devoted some of my research to interviewing graduates from the Naval Academy about this issue. One graduate had been a naval officer and had served ship duty during Vietnam.

"How do you explain the lack of a toleration clause?" I asked him.

"Well, it's damn tough. In a ship or a sub, you work very closely with a crew. You live very close to your shipmates. We must trust each other and it becomes difficult to do that when you think everybody is watching your every move and will tell on you if you miss something."

This represents the prevailing feeling arguing against a non-toleration clause. To my surprise, I found something completely different during the course of my research and interviews with other honorable leaders. Let me share a couple of quotes to illustrate where I'm going.

Captain Brian Wortinger remarked that the non-toleration clause actually protects the group or the team. When I presented him with this question, he answered it with a question: "What is it you're protecting in that team? What are the values of that team? If you're going to allow someone to undermine that, then we don't want them part of our team."

Dave Jones was passionate about this. "The organization is bigger than any individual. That's number one. Now that's too big of a concept for many people. But that's the truth. The bottom line is the mission and the organization is way above anything we should do."

Of all the people I interviewed, Lieutenant Colonel Blair Tiger may occupy the highest perch on the highest piece of the high ground. This former assistant to the West Point Commandant for all matters relating to honor reflected,

> The non-toleration clause is what glues our corporateness together. Without it we could have a body of rules, but there would not be the collective body of people that would have said, "You and I have a responsibility to live by these rules." It's the fellow-man-accountability component needed in any organization. Without it, it would just be an individual responsibility to follow the rules. Now it's *our* responsibility to follow the rules. In fact, it puts the *u* and the *s*, in us. It's what makes us, *us*.

As interesting as these sentiments were, what the 20-, 21-, and 22-year-old men and women said, was the most impressive. All cadets with whom I discussed the toleration clause were interviewed in a private setting where they could speak freely. I got the sense that sequestering these cadets was unnecessary; they would've spoken with candor in front of anybody.

Amy Wiershem is a talkative and strong-willed young woman. About toleration, she was quick to note that the way many cadets "are around here is that if somebody is truly your friend, they won't ever put you in that position [to tolerate] and that's what I've found."

When I talked to A. J. Bartone, a rising senior from California, he educated me on how the Honor Code, in general, and the non-toleration clause, in particular, has affected the nature and intimacy of his friendships.

> The Honor Code/system has really changed our friendship. He and I trust each other one hundred percent. And we have an understanding between each other that anything that we say to each other, anything we do...you know, it's all about the little things like he may want to borrow my car, that if he crashes it, or if he dings it, he'll let me know, he'll tell me. We have a deeper level of trust that doesn't exist with my friends back home.

Amy's and AJ's comments reflect a common pattern found within honorable relationships and within honorable organizations. Tolerating dishonorable acts of another never improves loyalty or cohesiveness. It will, in the long term, always damage relationships. In the

Dishonor will always erode loyalty.

end, loyalty based on dishonor will always erode. Just look at WorldCom and Enron where key players agreed to plead guilty and cooperate with the prosecution against their former bosses of Lay and Ebbers for more favorable sentences. This confirms that loyalty has boundaries. Honor does not.

The corollary is much more positive and it reflects the nature of honorable leadership. Not tolerating dishonorable decisions by friends actually improves the richness of the social relationship and will always lead to greater cohesion. This distinction is absolutely critical. While most people can imagine that not tolerating makes operating a ship more difficult, honorable leaders see zero toleration of dishonorable conduct as absolutely necessary to the efficient and safe functioning of that ship. Were that not the case, the United States Navy's "E" citation for excellence afloat would not be so highly coveted.

A fascinating characteristic of the friendship to honor relationship is that the variables are mutually reinforcing. Friendships can help protect and preserve another's honor backbone. We witnessed that when Bryan intervened and asked his buddy if he really wanted to lie to pick up his girlfriend. But the reverse is also true. Just as friendship can improve honor, honor can improve the quality, depth, and trust within a relationship. That is evident in AJ's quote above. The mutually reinforcing properties of this relationship make honor and social interaction an even more potent resource for those seeking to secure the high ground.

Finally, I want to call attention to a deeper problem here. While preserving loyalty is said to be the rationale used to tolerate certain acts of dishonor, it is not the true force behind tolerating acts that we know are just plain wrong. Abraham Lincoln once said, "To sin by silence when they should protest makes cowards out of men." Embedded in this statement is the real reason individuals tend to tolerate things that they know are wrong. Statements made by the recently promoted army major rang a bell for me, as there was something about toleration and honorable leaders that I was, to that point, missing: "It wasn't so much the loyalty that gave me pause ... that kept me silent. It wasn't so much about them, it was more about *me*. I wanted to be liked. Wanted to be popular. I guess what I wanted, in a tough environment like this [West Point], was to be accepted. If I told on them, I'd lose all of that."

Many years ago as a cadet, this major suffered from a weakness facing many leaders today, but one that true honorable leaders manage to overcome. He was willing to put his need to be liked, his need to be popular, ahead of his duty to do the right thing. None of this is easy. The need for inclusion is hardwired in all of us. Willingness to sacrifice popularity for doing what is honorable separates leaders in the valley from those leading from the high ground. Many, like Amy Wiershem, know that the people "watching her back" are themselves honorable, so she is less likely to be put in the position of sacrificing popularity for integrity. The conflict is hardly ever about loyalty. It is much more about a personal need to be liked above all else.

> *Honorable leaders will sacrifice popularity to preserve their integrity.*

WHISTLING "DIXIE"

If you think from the perspective that a culture of honor actually improves, never detracts, from loyalty, we should see whistleblowing in a new light. Frank Serpico does. Frank Serpico was shot by a drug dealer and left to die by his fellow New York City police officers who many believe had colluded with the drug dealer to keep Serpico from exposing widespread police corruption. In 1971, Serpico survived and became what he called a lamplighter, not a whistleblower, by testifying for the Knapp Commission investigating corruption within the New York City police force. Serpico prefers the notion of a "lamplighter"[9] in the spirit of Paul Revere's "midnight ride" that illuminated the truth—the British were, indeed, coming. Lamplighters shed light and expose the truth and help defeat corruption, graft, and deceit otherwise concealed by darkness from the public.

I came to see the tremendous application of this lamplighting metaphor when I revisited some historical examples. A particularly vivid example is Daniel Ellsberg, a former State Department analyst, who leaked *The Pentagon Papers* in 1971. *The Pentagon Papers* revealed the inept, corrupt, and deceitful foreign policy of previous presidential administrations and is credited with sparking a stiff and unrelenting public resistance to the Vietnam War.[10]

Cynthia Cooper of WorldCom, Sherron Watkins of Enron, and Collen Rowledy of the FBI, all lighted a lamp that exposed serious organizational shortcomings. For that, the three were selected as *Time's* People of the Year in 2002.[11] From observing them and hearing them speak, they too appear to be unassuming and somewhat uncomfortable with their own notoriety.

> *Honor is more about light than about a whistle. Things dangerous in the dark are often quite safe when there is light.*

Teams, groups, and organizations need to be "well lit." Lamplighters make sure that the lights in your vehicle are on at night as you approach a *moment*. The clever thing about this is that headlights protect you, pedestrians, and other drivers. Thus, lamplighting must be encouraged, never discouraged, since it protects all interested parties.

SOCIAL GRACES

Many believe that the key to making an impact on somebody's honor is one-way communication. Indeed, much of the training on leadership and honor seems to be academic and conducted in classroom settings. Even at West Point, cadets are exposed to 47 hours of classes during their 4 years to enrich each cadet's capacity to lead honorably. While this type of training does improve one's honor backbone, I don't think it's nearly as effective as you may expect. There are natural limitations to the artificial setting of a workshop or a classroom. It is again the uniquely social side of honorable leadership that best explains how people really develop their honor backbones that enable them to reach the high ground.

One young man I interviewed at West Point describes his communication patterns:

> If you sit around with drinks at West Point long enough, you'll end up talking about either something that happened in Iraq or some sort of ethical dilemma. It may not be right away, but it's going to come up eventually. When I go home and I go visit my buddies at school, it never happens, it never comes up. I think by forcing us to discuss it here, whenever you get in a heated debate, you never want to end it. You always want to continue this debate, so you'll develop it outside of the hour-long classroom. If you don't give them that chance to discuss it, then it's never going to come up over a beer. It's never going to come up while you're watching a game.

I asked another senior officer if he mentors any young men and women at West Point. His initial response is intriguing, "And when they come over to our house … even when we're feeding them chips and salsa, they will talk about ways to role model or they will present some ethics-oriented ideas."

Both of these statements are entertaining and informative. The first lesson is that principles of honorable leadership are best transferred not in a one-way telling fashion. Two-way, interactive learning is more appropriate to capture and transfer the essence of honorable leadership. That much is easy. It is the second lesson, to me, that is much more intriguing.

Until now, this book has focused almost exclusively on questions relating to the *how*. For example, I argue that *Going All In!* and *Being Big About Small Things* are tactics that tell you *how* to make it to the summit. What is particularly interesting, however, is that in explaining how they learned or taught honorable leadership, both the West Point cadet and senior faculty member honed in on the *where*.

> *The context or the where is of critical importance in the development of honorable leaders.*

The *why* and *how* are important. But *where* people talk and learn about honorable leadership is a function of *how* well and *how* quickly they learn. Put plainly, the *where* is pretty damned important. And notice again, that there is some social component to all of this. Undeniably, there are some social graces at work in becoming an honorable leader.

Not that we should be at all surprised. Reflect about the best road trips that you've ever been on. Chances are that the best times occurred when you pulled off the side of the road and had a picnic. Or went off the beaten path to a small, quaint restaurant. Maybe it was at a nice bed and breakfast somewhere. We tend to remember and we hold dear the stops we make on our trips. It is these intimate and deeply social moments where we learn and appreciate the most. The same can be said for the practice of honorable leadership. The best way to prepare for a *moment* or an intersection is to take a moment. Classroom education is needed, but it is only a small step toward the high ground. Where people learn the most about honorable leadership is outside of the classroom, in non-threatening environments, where social friendships emerge and take over and where the teacher–student or boss–supervisor relationship seems to melt away. The takeaway from all this is to not abandon traditional modes of learning, but to supplement that learning in an environment conducive to social interaction. This is where the real secrets of securing the high ground are held.

We've just learned that there is moral power in social interaction. Having the right people at the right time to "watch your back" is clearly instrumental in the climb to the summit. But here we may be stuck. People often remark to me that it takes 10 units of effort to arrive at an 80 percent solution. To get from 80 to 95 or to 100 often requires 100 units of effort—10 times the effort to get to 80. Currently, we are at the 80 percent watermark. The remaining climb to the high ground will be difficult. However, it may be a bit easier if we decide to use our imagination.

7

Imagine That

Reality leaves a lot to the imagination.

—John Lennon

WE MUST PROTECT THIS HOUSE!

That is the mantra of Under Armour sports apparel. This company has recorded a growth rate of more than 133 percent from 2000 to 2005, and was founded by Kevin Plank, a former linebacker and special teams player at the University of Maryland. Plank started Under Armour in the basement of his grandmother's house after he grew weary of wearing heavy, traditional, cotton T-shirts under his football pads. With no textile or science experience, Plank believed that a special fabric existed or could be made that would wick moisture away from the body without making the garment sweat-stained or water-heavy—a common problem of the widely used cotton material. His hunch was right. Plank's entrepreneurial dream, which began in his grandma's basement with $40,000 in credit card, cash advances and debt, is no longer a dream. With annual sales of over $240 million as of June 30, 2005, the dream is now a reality.[1]

Consider the "Fosbury Flop." Dick Fosbury was no ordinary athlete. At the 1968 Olympic games in Mexico City he joined the other high jumpers out on the track. When his turn came to do the high jump, he surprised a lot of people and, in the process, revolutionized a track event that had not changed in hundreds of years. Rather than leaping facing the bar and swinging one leg and then the other over the bar in a scissorslike motion like everyone else, Dick Fosbury turned just as he jumped. He then flung his body *backward* over the bar with his back in an arch. He followed with his legs and landed on his shoulders—a technique now commonly referred to as the Fosbury Flop. This approach was not only innovative but also effective. In fact, he won the gold medal and set a new Olympic record. His tactic is now so mainstream that most track athletes do not even know the way it was done before Fosbury stepped onto the field in 1968.[2]

These examples show what can happen when a single individual decides to use his or her imagination. Whether an entrepreneur, an artist, or even an athlete, imagination is an important variable in making the average, good, and the good, great. Examining the truly brilliant products and ideas of history finds imagination present in every case. From Bill Walsh and the West-coast Offense to Woodrow Wilson and the League of Nations. From Henry Ford and the assembly line to Eli Whitney and the cotton gin. Or from REM and alternative rock to Larry Page and Sergey Brin of Google. Regardless of the field or specialty, greatness requires innovation and imagination. Accordingly, I sought in my research to understand if there is room for imagination in the act of leading honorably. The answer to that question is an undeniable Yes. I found that the same imagination that enables entrepreneurs, artists, and musicians to design and build great products and works of art is used by honorable leaders to build their honor backbones. Imagination was highly correlated with leader elevation—those actively using their imaginations led from the high ground. Those with a shallow or inactive imagination could be found in the valleys.

> To reach the high elevation, rely on the imagination.

PICK A HERO!

It is Okay to admit that one of your favorite movies is Kevin Bacon's *Footloose*. Nobody is going to make fun of you for that confession. Not only was that movie a launching point for Kevin Bacon, its soundtrack ignited the careers of several, now famous, music artists. Kenny Loggins, Sammy Hagar, and Quiet Riot all have *Footloose* to thank for energizing their careers. Less known on that list, but coming at the most critical time in the movie, was the song "Holding Out for a Hero" by Bonnie Tyler. In this ballad, Bonnie Tyler laments that it is just damn tough to find a hero. What's more is she's losing hope and that her survival, her ability to carry on is in jeopardy because either she can't find a hero or they can't find her. No doubt, this is a sad song with a sadder message—where are the heroes in this world when I need them most?

I chose this song not so much because I just loved it when I heard it twenty something years ago in *Footloose*. I chose it to reflect a problem that rarely occurs at West Point or within organizations led by honorable leaders where no one is ever holding out for a hero. It seems that, on the ascent to the

> Heroes help make the trek to the high ground doable.

high ground, all that one can see are heroes. And as Bonnie Tyler seems to readily understand, heroes are special and important, and without them it becomes difficult to reach the summit. Aspiring leaders tend to pick one of these heroes and *imagine* being just like them.

Make and Model

The most pervasive and "in your face" message during my research was the importance of these heroes since they become role models for others to follow. The heroes at West Point are both living and dead. Statues of Eisenhower, MacArthur, Washington, and Patton dot the West Point campus. Guest speakers include the likes of former Secretary of State Colin Powell, Coach K of Duke, and General Norman Schwarzkopf. These famous leaders are certainly powerful role models for our imaginations. Also essential are the not-so-famous role models that aspiring, high-ground leaders look to.

When asked about this, Lieutenant Colonel Dave Jones of the Simon Center almost leaped out of his seat:

> This is a hard business [to build honorable leaders]. But the bottom line is, I think, role models have to be number one. I think the chemistry instructor, the math instructor, the English instructor, what they say when the door is closed is huge. It's unbelievable. But everything they say is being absorbed, I promise. And how about the coach? The bottom line is that sometimes the coaches have more influence; it's kind of like parental influence.

I was about to jump in, but Dave refused to stop.

> What are we doing at West Point? Ninety percent of our faculty rotates every three years. We turn them over. Who are the people we're getting in for instructors here? They're great role models from the army. That's the single most important purpose for they're being brought here. They're not even great teachers. They're not subject matter experts. That all comes because of our work ethic, we come here and become good teachers. Maybe not great teachers, by the way, but we better be great role models. If you have one bad one [role model], it sticks in your mind and you ask, "How did that happen?"

During the course of my research, one of the most sophisticated, complex, and morally sound persons I met was a 22-year-old young man who, ironically, committed an honor violation during his first semester at West Point.

During his first semester, some upperclassmen were playing rough in the name of school spirit during or just around a big football game. These upperclassmen had gotten a bunch of plebes together in a room and started shoving them around and this one young man got hit in the eye. The hit left a bruise. None of this behavior is acceptable in any organization, including

West Point. So the cadet first sergeant, a young woman not more than 22 years old, started asking around and she came to this young man with the bruised eye. She asked him how he had gotten it. To protect his friends and to protect the upperclassmen from sure punishment, he lied and told her that he fell and bruised it himself. She said Okay and walked away. This young man, who, by the way, could've gone to any college in the nation, thought about what he said over the weekend and revisited the unsuspecting first sergeant on Monday where he told her that he lied—he had, indeed, been hit in the face. This young man was found guilty of an honor violation.

Fifteen years ago, this young man would've been kicked out of West Point for violating the Honor Code. However, West Point's Superintendent thought that this young man still held potential and could be mentored to overcome this setback and to get back on track to becoming a great leader. On the basis of the Superintendent's guidance, this young man was enrolled in the honor mentorship program. The honor mentorship program is a 6-month program where a young man or woman is paired with another West Point officer who, incidentally, is a great role model. In addition to the assigning of a role model, the *United States Corps of Cadets Honor System and Procedures* requires additional components of the mentorship character development program:

- **Counseling.** Attend bi-monthly counseling sessions with the mentor.
- **Journal.** Learn to reflect and assess by putting thoughts to paper.
- **X/Y case.** Write an X/Y case, which I'll describe below, in the first person.
- **Honor class.** Teach part or all of an honor class to other cadets.
- **Development project.** Create, design, and implement a developmental project.
- **Role model.** The core of the program.
- **Summary essay.** Write an essay that summarizes the developmental experience.

The fascinating aspect of this program and what makes it so effective is the heavy reliance on imagination. At each step, imagination is involved. In this scenario, the young man who had violated the Honor Code was paired with a major in the U. S. Army. You may be wondering what the impact this program had on this young man. When I interviewed him, he was one of a privileged few selected as a cadet company commander during his senior year. He grew from relying on a role model to becoming one himself. In fact, he was an enthusiastic participant in teaching honor education to other, junior leaders. During interviews with other West Point cadets, administrators, faculty, and staff, many often referred to this young man as what every young leader should strive, or imagine, to become. The presence of role models was instrumental in catapulting this young man from the valley to the summit. It is important to note that we don't have to experience an honor setback before we use our imaginations.

The interaction of two critical variables made this success story possible: imagination and role models. Role models fulfill multiple functions. Role models are a physical manifestation of abstract principles, such as honor, integrity, ethics, or leadership. Discussing these principles in a sterile classroom is one thing, but seeing them applied by someone is totally different. It is the difference between telling and showing. Telling an aspiring leader what honor is, has obvious limitations. Those limitations are curbed when an individual can actually see what an honorable leader looks and acts like. In addition to personally demonstrating the application of principles, role models serve a much more mundane purpose—great role models can also be models of efficiency. Because role models are already on the high ground, they have already cleared a path for us to follow. Norman Schwarzkopf is famous for saying that you should never repaint the flagpole if it already has a fresh coat of paint. The parallel for aspiring leaders is that it makes little sense to blaze our own new path to the summit when our role models have already cleared a path for us. We all know that making it to the high ground is a difficult enough endeavor. That endeavor becomes substantially easier when a hero is already there to show us the way.

The use of imagination is straightforward. Once we identify a hero, we do our part by imagining ourselves as that person. Closely related to this aspect of imagination is the notion of aspiration. Through imagination and a role model as a benchmark, we can aspire to a higher level. Without imagination or role models, aspiring to be better or to do better, would be a climb too steep for many to

> *When imagination is used with role models, the result is aspiration.*

manage alone. The lesson here is to pick one or more role models and imagine yourself at their level. There is, perhaps, no more efficient approach to the high ground.

COLD CASE

Cold cases are not good things in law enforcement. Cold cases are crimes that, for whatever reason, have never been solved. Dead end leads, weak witnesses, or sloppy investigations, all contribute to a case going "cold." Once a case becomes cold, it often becomes forgotten and it is tough to make it "hot" again.

One of the hallmarks of honorable leaders and respectable organizations is neither permits a case to become "cold." Nowhere is this more evident at West Point than in the publication of the *Hip Pocket Values Guide* (2004 edition). This publication is 4 inches by 7 inches and contains only 40 pages. That is for a reason—it can fit in about any pocket and can be taken most anywhere. Those 40 pages provide a strong competitive advantage to any individual wishing to secure the high ground.

Inside this *Hip Pocket Guide* are several X/Y cases. X/Y cases are actual events, usually written about by those involved in the honor process, describing cadet honor offenses that actually occurred at West Point. All involve a rise or fall in elevation. By their very nature, they're West Point's equivalent of a cold case, but by continuously learning and discussing them, these cases never die or get cold. I include an actual case from the *Hip Pocket Guide* to provide a fuller appreciation of the value of West Point's version of a cold case.

> Cadet Doe and his buddies Smith and Jones are sophomores who, without taking leave, left post one night and went out drinking. The trip appeared to be a success (to the cadets) until they returned to West Point, just before TAPS [bed check]. On their way across Central Area, the Officer-in-Charge (OC), Captain Strac, noticed the three cadets talking loudly and walking with apparently great difficulty. Upon approaching them it was clearly evident they were intoxicated and the OC asked them what they had been drinking. Cadet Doe replied that they had been drinking Coke, when in fact they had all been drinking rum and Coke.

The case doesn't end there, however. It asks us to do some investigating, to use our imaginations. It asks, How does Cadet Doe's statement relate to the definition of "quibbling" or equivocation—the telling of only a partial truth? Then it prods us to think how the Three Rules of Thumb could be used to help shape our response.

These cases are extremely valuable because they force leaders to use their imaginations to become Cadet Doe, Cadet Smith, or Cadet Jones. Using imagination and putting themselves in the midst of the true-to-life circumstances, they can imagine how they'd respond or what choices they'd face. The beauty of these X/Y cases rests in its trigger effect on our imaginations. We can't help but feel empathy, concern, pressure, and the sensation and the surprise of being caught. Consequently, this "imagination trigger" causes us to perform a mental simulation—a learning practice that is almost as good as being there in the actual scenario. How much better might our leaders and organizations be if they learned from another's victories or setbacks? This point is so central to reaching the high ground, it warrants further discussion.

Strike Up the Bandura!

To more fully appreciate the impact of cold cases and role models, we need to understand how people learn. Professor Ruth Kanfer, an expert in managerial and organizational learning, has a good definition of learning that is apropos to what we're talking about here. According to Kanfer, learning is a relatively permanent change in the frequency of occurrence of a particular behavior, which, in our case, is honorable behavior.[3]

One of the early, and dominant, schools of thought on how people go about learning was that of "operant conditioning." Coined by the famous psychologist B.F. Skinner, operant conditioning refers to a process whereby we learn through consequence, usually some type of reward or punishment. A child that learns not to touch a hot stove through a slap on the wrist or positive reinforcement in the form of praise from a coach are both examples of operant conditioning—learning by consequence. Many of B.F. Skinner's experiments were initially done on how rats would learn to do certain things to earn a food pellet. Well, we're not rats and the overriding assumption behind this approach is that you must personally be involved or experience a consequence for yourself to be able to learn.

Enter Albert Bandura, another social psychologist. Bandura developed an alternative view of learning, which he named social "cognitive theory." This theory differed from Skinner's in that a major thrust of this perspective is that we can learn through cognitive processing. We can learn a new behavior by watching others in any given situation and then choosing to imitate or not to imitate that behavior.[4]

This concept of learning by example is ruthlessly exploited by honorable leaders. Rather than repeating the same mistakes themselves, they learn from others, either through role models or cold cases. This tactic tends to be effective. It is costly to repeat mistakes while it is always beneficial to learn best practices by observing another person, group, or organization. For honorable leaders, reaching the high ground is

> *Honorable leaders learn from the experiences of others.*

almost equal parts doing and observing. The best place to bear witness to the power of social cognitive theory is to return to West Point's mentorship and character development program. Here, reflection, imagination, and imitation of high ground role models are critical.

I ALWAYS FEEL LIKE SOMEBODY'S WATCHING ME

In the mid 1980s, a musician named Rockwell sang a song, "Somebody's Watching Me," which, luckily for him, had guest cameos by Michael and Jermaine Jackson. This song that rocketed up the charts (and right out of our lives) featured a video of Rockwell walking through his house which he believed was haunted by fictitious movie characters, the IRS, and, most dangerous, the mailman. I invite you to go ahead and google Rockwell to see for yourself the powerful paranoia that must've overtaken poor Rockwell. The *CliffsNotes* version is as the name suggests. Rockwell always thought that somebody was watching him.

A rather extraordinary event occurred in the basement of Lincoln Hall on the West Point post on March 5, 2004. Lincoln Hall is the home of West Point's social science department, a department that is full of officers sent back to receive graduate degrees in public policy and economics from such places as Harvard, Stanford, MIT, and Columbia. Even for an academy graduate, Lincoln Hall is an intimidating place where cadets experience one of the army's premiere think tanks for strategic defense policy. It is here that I met Major Mike Yankovich. Mike Yankovich graduated among the top of his West Point class back in 1994 and was selected by the army to pursue graduate studies in economics at Duke. At the time of my interview with Mike, he was just transitioning out of his position as an economics instructor. When the issue of honorable leadership came up, Mike reached into his desk drawer and shared with me a memorandum for record that detailed the events that occurred on March 5, 2004. The case involved a young man who had come to Mike's office to take a make-up quiz just before he was to leave for spring break. Here is a brief excerpt from this memorandum:

> The quiz is worth 50 points. The quiz requires cadets to use their personal laptop computers and Microsoft Excel to solve a "net present value analysis" problem. When Cadet XXX came to my office at approximately 0945 hours on March 5, 2004, I instructed him to get his laptop out, turn it on, and open the file that contained a shell for the quiz. The quiz shell file was a password-protected file that I sent to all cadets who would be taking the quiz. Cadet XXX said that he did not have the file on his laptop. I then allowed him to copy the file from my CD-R onto his desktop. I then verbally instructed Cadet XXX that there were no authorized references for the quiz and that the only file that he was allowed to have open on his laptop was the file for the quiz shell.

Mike then left the cadet to complete the quiz. While Mike was in and out of his office, there was little to no supervision of this young man. Lincoln Hall was quiet while the post prepared for spring break. The story is not over.

> After Cadet XXX finished taking the quiz, he told me that he was done and that he saved the updated file to his desktop. He did not have a floppy disk and the wireless system was not working in the building so I told him to return to his room and e-mail the quiz file to me as soon as he got back to his room. I then left my office and Cadet XXX began putting on his outer garments.

> When I came back, Cadet XXX stopped me in the hall just outside my office. He told me that he forgot about the verbal instructions not to use any references. He then told me that he used a reference to look up how to calculate the discount factor as part of the quiz.

I asked Major Yankovich about the particulars of this case.

"Would you say that he was supervised while taking this quiz?"

"Not at all. He was by himself, for the most part."

I pressed, "If he had not told you about this, what were the chances that he would've been caught cheating?"

Mike responded quickly, "Zero. There was no way this young man would've been caught. None at all. He could've gotten away with it and would've gotten a B or A on the quiz. Nobody would've ever known, except him. Despite a zero percent chance of being caught, he decided to tell me anyway."

"What grade did he get?"

"He failed. And a preliminary honor investigation was launched. The fact that he wasn't paying very good attention when I gave him the instructions and, in essence, forgot what I said to him coupled with his self-report indicated that he had not consciously demonstrated intent to cheat. He was found to be careless, but not dishonorable. Actually, the fact that he told me when nobody but him would've ever known illustrates just how honorable this young man was. But he still failed the quiz."

Just to check, I asked, "So, what you are telling me is that, essentially, this guy told on himself despite knowing that there was absolutely no way that he was going to be caught. And, on top of that, he knew that he was going to get a D or F on the quiz and risk an honor investigation by telling you?"

"Yep. Kind of amazing isn't it?"

As Mike finished this story, I couldn't help think that this story was more about Roswell than it was about Rockwell, the paranoid singer. Roswell, New Mexico, of course, is the place of the mysterious UFO sightings and alleged alien landings in 1947. Having earned my doctorate in business, my cynical side kicked in. I thought that this case of a 21-year-old man making the decisions that he did was as inexplicable as the Roswell UFO sightings. It doesn't often happen. As I talked to Mike about this case, my hypothesis about this event became less Roswell and more Rockwell.

We've already highlighted in Chapter 6 that we behave much differently when other people are around us or when we know we're being observed. Think about your behavior when your boss steps into the room. I have two good friends who sell pharmaceuticals. When their district manager rides with them on their visits to doctor offices and hospitals, both remark about how professional they become or how their "face" changes when they are with their district manager. They play different radio stations, talk less on their cell phones, keep personal cell calls to a minimum, and take shorter lunch breaks. Although our behavior changes to a slight degree when we're around our boss, friends, spouse, parents, or employees, the setting in which we find ourselves may be even more important in sparking a change in behavior. Our tone, style, and mannerisms are different when we're in a church compared to a locker room or tailgate at a football game. I bring this up because it explains why this young man chose to take a step toward the high ground.

After hearing this case, I was unable to interview the young man, but I interviewed several other cadets, faculty, staff, and working professionals about the details of what happened here and I asked them to help me explain this phenomenon. What could explain why a young man would do the counterintuitive, but honorable, action of telling on himself when there was no way that he was going to be caught? The answer lies in the principle of imagination. What this young man and others like him do, is to actually pretend that others are watching them. Taking a page out of Rockwell, they believe that somebody they respect, such as a role model, is actually sitting beside them when they're not. Honorable leaders understand that we act differently when we know people are watching. When nobody is actually around, they engage their imagination to pretend that somebody is. And, for honorable leadership, this makes all the difference in the world.

> *When confronting a difficult moment, pretend that a role model is watching you.*

PLAY TIME!

Counterfactual history is fun and controversial. Counterfactual or "alternative" historians ask the What-if questions. They may ask "What if the United States would have dropped the nuclear bomb on Germany, rather than Japan?" or "What if General Lee would have decided not to take the fight to the North in June 1863 and had not stumbled on July 1st into the Battle of Gettysburg?" or, more recently, "What if we would have acted on intelligence before September 11, 2001, that members of Al-Qaeda were attending flight schools in Florida in preparation for an attack?" The use of counterfactual thinking is quite prevalent. The commission that looked at the voting problems in Florida during the 2000 presidential election is a classic case of examining an event that happened in the past and then asking What-if questions to generate present day lessons. In reality, we tend to be preoccupied with the "what if" question. A great example of this preoccupation can be found at WhatIfSports.com where you can play around with outcomes using players from different eras. For instance, what would be the outcome if Babe Ruth would've stayed with the Boston Red Sox and Pedro Martinez was born 100 years ago and ended up playing for the Yankees against the Babe. Or what if former Maryland basketball star, Len Bias, never died of a cocaine overdose and joined the Boston Celtics with Bird, Ainge, McHale, and Parrish, as he was drafted to do? How many more banners would've flown in the Boston Garden if only Len Bias had never died? We can see that this counterfactual thinking can be quite complex, sophisticated, and tangled. But, in almost every case, the What-if questions are past-oriented and backward thinking.

Then there is Nostradamus, who lived in the early 1500s in France. Trained as a physician and astrologer, Nostradamus is most famous for his collection of prophecies. Nostradamus wielded tremendous power, not because he looked to the past, but rather, because he focused on the future. In 1555, he wrote *Centuries*, a rather imaginative collection of very general predictions that some argue predicted the San Francisco earthquakes, the assassination of President Kennedy, and even the attacks on the World Trade Center. Even back then, many French citizens were fascinated with his prophecies and would travel to Salon, France, to meet Nostradamus in the hope of gaining insight into their own futures. Indeed, Catherine de Medici, the queen of France at the time, requested that Nostradamus generate horoscopes for her husband, King Henry II, and their children. Shortly thereafter, King Charles IX of France anointed Nostradamus the royal physician.[5] Whereas counterfactual historians and the like gain pleasure from reexamining the past, Nostradamus gained his pleasure and power from looking at the future. Unlike counterfactual historians, Nostradamus and those like him don't ask "What if?" They describe the future as they see it.

I raise these different cases and personalities to illustrate a fact. There is a tendency to gain insight from either reliving the past or predicting the future. Most people don't do both. Honorable leaders do. The honorable leaders whom I interviewed clearly think in a manner that integrates past- and future-oriented learning techniques, which capitalize on the strengths while eliminating the shortcomings of each. Picture a counterfactual Nostrodamus; that is what honorable leaders are. In a dangerous *moment*, they are able to project themselves into the future like Nostrodamus. Then they look in the rear view mirror at this *moment* or intersection and ask, "What if?" Those who lead from the high ground marry the what-if characteristic of counterfactual historians in a future-oriented way. Honorable leaders skillfully and imaginatively play with the notion of time in a manner that strengthens their honor backbones and helps them climb toward the summit. I'd like to investigate how they go about playing with time when they exploit what I call a rearview mirror tactic and TIVO approach to decision-making.

> *Those on the high ground combine the "what ifs" of the past with the possibilities of the future.*

Remember Robert Smith, the plebe who had failed English and was stuck at summer school? During our interview, I expected him to say that he was upset and bitter at being confined to West Point during the summer. Upon reflection, he acknowledged that he could've easily cheated several times during the normal semester and, by so doing, would've probably received a passing grade and would not have been in summer school. His response was quite different and profound: "If you cheat you're taking away from yourself and I wouldn't have learned what I needed to learn about English composition." He elaborated that English composition would be important in the future when he was trying to communicate to his soldiers, his peers, and his superiors as an army officer.

Cadet Smith is illustrative of this rearview mirror tactic of decision-making. This 19-year-old cadet was going through a *moment* and pretending that he didn't successfully navigate it because he had cheated his way through plebe English. He then projected far into the future and asked the "What-if" questions, which powerfully evoked the consequences if he had never learned to write—he wouldn't be able to communicate and he would be ineffective as a leader. Leaders in the valley lack the mental sophistication or discipline to embrace the rearview mirror approach. Many would've dealt with the here and now and cheated their way through English just to get a grade and move on to the next course. These same people would have given little thought to medium- or long-term consequences of their decisions. If you think of how this young man made his decision, you see that honorable leaders deal with the tension of time—past, present, and future—in a way that leaders in lower elevations cannot.

Sarah Dome, an enthusiastic young West Point soccer player, struck me as an honorable leader. She demonstrated her ability to project forward and look back through her rearview mirror:

> We've heard about a senior who was kicked out his senior year for a paper that he cheated on during his sophomore year. So you think about everything you're turning in now. There's a chance that somebody in the future may borrow it to build upon your thoughts or research. If they use it and it's not documented right, you could still get in trouble. What is worse, you're worried about everything you're doing now, and you're concerned about your possible exposure in the future.

Her thoughts reflect a recurring theme of honorable leaders. Often they are able to keep one eye on the present or past while keeping another eye on the horizon. One of the positive consequences of this approach is balanced decision-making that is aware of the need for urgency on one hand while acknowledging the long-term consequences on the other.

Closely related to this idea of the rearview mirror method is what I call the "TIVO effect." A TIVO device can record every episode of your favorite television show and can actually control live TV. By pushing a button, you can pause, rewind, slo-mo, instant replay, and, amazingly, fast-forward through boring parts of a movie or a commercial. With the TIVO, you, not the network, control time.

A great deal of effort at West Point and, I think, in the development of honorable leaders in other organizations, aims to make leaders like human TIVOs. This is difficult since many people get caught up in a *moment*. Getting swept away by a *moment* doesn't have to be.

I sat down with a colonel who volunteers his time as a member of a values education team (VET) that discusses honorable leadership with cadets. Regarding imagination, time, and the TIVO effect, he noted:

> I think we do a lot of that [imagination] here in our values education training. We try to get cadets to put themselves in a situation here and think down the road. [We ask,] "What are the impacts of your decision here?" And we branch out. How does this decision made today affect people in the future. A lot of times you can make a decision without much thought that it has tremendous consequences. And that's why we always emphasize with cadets that those decisions that you make are very important. In essence, all decisions are important. Even if you think they have minor consequences, they could have major impacts.

Being conscious of a rearview mirror and the TIVO way of thinking assures that honorable leaders remain mindful of the probable and unforeseen consequences of their decisions. In his tragic and haunting short story "Soldier's Home" about a World War I combat veteran who has come home spiritually emptied by the war, Ernest Hemingway said of the shell-shocked Harold Krebs, "He did not want any consequences. He did not want any consequences ever again. He wanted to live along without consequences." Reliance upon rearview mirror and TIVO thinking reminds honorable leaders that one might be able to live without consequences, but one can never *lead* without consequences.

Your TIVO Is Never Rated R!

To summarize where we've just been, we've discussed the rearview mirror and TIVO approach to honorable decision-making. The rearview approach involves projecting yourself into the future, and then looking back into the past through the rear mirror to see what the ramifications would have been *if* you went with a particular decision. TIVO involves the manipulation of time, either speeding up, slowing down, or pausing, as we approach a *moment*.

Both approaches have the power to defeat the R-word. Remember, the R-word attempts to find a rationalization for a decision or action that is wrong. The R-word works through a variety of ways as discussed in Chapter 3. One of its more potent mechanisms is to psychologically create distance between the decision and its consequences. One particularly powerful way to keep the R-word from working havoc is to embrace the rearview and TIVO tactics for honorable decision-making. The rearview tactic of asking "What would the intersection or *moment* look like in my rearview mirror if I acted dishonorably?" steadies our focus on consequences. What I'm saying here is that if leaders use the rearview mirror approach to honorable decision-making, they cannot ignore consequences. And when consequences aren't ignored, the R-word dies.

Like the rearview mirror, the TIVO does not like things rated R. Another hallmark of the R-word is its creation of a false sense of urgency surrounding a *moment*. The R-word erodes our ability to reason by tricking us into believing that the brakes are out and the lights don't work, so we have to make an immediate decision to survive. This doesn't work on the highway and it does not work for honorable leadership. Turning the car to the left or right as you approach a *moment* takes you off the road to an area more dangerous since it isn't paved. So, the best bet will always be to slow down, stop, or put on your bright lights to see through and beyond the intersection. That is what the human TIVO function does. It says that it is Okay to stop, to slow down, to look at this *moment* more carefully and with greater precision. Using the fast-forward function is like the rearview method: a leader can imagine how this *moment* will turn out. It is possible with a TIVO device to skip ahead one scene or to the very end of the episode.

This fast-forward mechanism sparks the imagination to think about all kinds of consequences—immediate, mid, or long term. For that reason when installing the TIVO in ourselves, we no longer get tricked into making a decision that is artificially urgent. Only in the rarest cases are people going to die if a decision is not made within seconds. A key to remember is that we always have more time than we think and the TIVO reinforces that concept since *we* control the time. With a TIVO, you're in control. When control is located squarely in the leader's hands, the R-word no longer can work its evil magic since with control comes responsibility and accountability—the very things that the R-word tries to prevent. Sadly, one of the universal findings at West Point is that procrastination, and procrastination's false sense of urgency, is the number one reason men and women fall from the high ground. So argue Lieutenant Colonels Blair Tiger and Dave Jones, both experts in the West Point honor system.

> *Be like a TIVO: you control time. Never let time control you.*

Equipped with a rearview mirror and TIVO, this becomes unlikely, if not impossible. That is why honorable leaders and honorable organizations encourage, not restrain, a person's imagination to become one part counterfactual historian and one part Nostradamus. That type of thinking is critical if one wants a "no glare" rearview mirror and a risk-free trial of TIVO. A mental and imaginative rearview mirror and TIVO can change our lives, and it affects how we lead.

Split Personality

It is difficult to imagine former TYCO CEO Dennis Kozlowski spending $6,000 of TYCO funds on a shower curtain if he had used his mental rearview mirror or TIVO. Paul Volcker was the former Federal Reserve Board Chairman commissioned to investigate the corruption within the United Nations (UN) and related corporations in the UN's oil for food program in Iraq during the 1990s. Volcker's study revealed that these people used their positions, or offered and accepted bribes, to exploit a humanitarian program for personal financial gain.[6] How much different would their decisions have been if these politicians, lobbyists, and high-level executives would've used their rearview mirrors or TIVOs.

Early in my research, I recognized that those who lead from the high ground are decidedly different from those who toil at lower elevations. Those who lead from the high ground use the future and the past to deal with the present. Those that lead from the high ground rely upon imagination to make sense of a difficult reality. What is of particular interest and is fraught with contradiction is the development of powerful imaginations. Next time out, look about and assess which demographic possesses the richest imagination. To me, this demographic can be found on playgrounds, watching Blue's Clues, or taking a fanciful nap in kindergarten. With most people, imaginations are most active in their very early years. An inverse relationship is at work here. For the vast majority, as they age, their imagination weakens. Not so for honorable leaders at West Point and beyond. When plebes first enter West Point, they are preoccupied with rules, and rules only. They are afraid of violating the Honor Code. In reality, there is no real reason to fear the Honor Code. In 1971, Cadet Captain Patrick Finnegan (current Dean of the Academic Board—Brigadier General Finnegan) said, "A man has nothing to fear from the Honor Code as long as he lives honorably." Those words still ring true today, for men and women alike. But the point here is that early on in a cadet's development there is no real imagination at work. But, as they progress and climb in elevation, a moral imagination takes hold and grows.

We are within shouting distance of the top, the pinnacle, the summit—the high ground.

To clear the hump and to finally secure and Stand Your Ground requires all of us to carefully examine how we're wired and to do something that will feel uncomfortable, and, no doubt, unnatural. The last few yards can be conquered by encouraging and by prodding our innovation, creativity, and imagination. The majority of leaders on the high ground are made whole and complete through their imaginations.

So close your eyes. When I count to three, I would like you to *imagine* what it must be like to be on the top. To be on the high ground. When I snap my fingers, you'll be a new and different leader. You'll be on the high ground. Are you ready? One... Two...

8

Views From the Top

Age wrinkles the body. Quitting wrinkles the soul.
—General Douglas MacArthur

The views are terrific from the top, on the high ground. Before you fix your gaze on the majestic vistas, I encourage you first to look to your immediate left and immediate right. I can assure you that you're in great company, but it may not be quite what you'd expect.

To read media accounts and watch Hollywood movies, there is often only one type of leader. The leaders whom we see in films possess some remarkable qualities. To be sure, most are incredibly attractive and dashing. The celluloid leader whom we have in our minds is a dynamic speaker who radiates charisma. The Hollywood leader is at his or her best during times of crisis when he or she can flex muscles and exercise power. A classic movie that seems to encompass all off these characteristics is the widely forgotten 1988, sci-fi *They Live*. In this movie, Rowdy Roddy Piper, a classic hero from the early days of Vince McMahon's World Wrestling Federation (WWF), stumbles upon some magic sunglasses that give him the power to see aliens among the general population. As he confronts some of these aliens, he sticks out his chest and says, "I've come here to chew bubblegum and kick ass. And I'm all out of bubblegum." This may sorely disappoint you, but you will not see that type of person on the high ground. That type of leader may exist elsewhere, but not on the summit.

The air is cool, clear, and crisp up here on the high ground. The views unobstructed. Under these ideal conditions, we can use our clarity of vision to see what great leaders really are and to see, firsthand, the many misconceptions that surround this thing we call leadership.

NANCY DREW MEETS THE HARDY BOYS

I had mentioned earlier that my oldest daughter, Madison, was on a Nancy Drew marathon. Interestingly, her marathon seemed to begin at about the same time I started this research project. Oddly enough, the patterns, the ebbs and flows of her reading seemed to correspond almost exactly to the patterns, ebbs and flows of my own research. When I wanted to take a break, she, too, was looking for a rest. She would then approach me to ask if I'd read to her a while. Before I knew it, we had closed the chapter on such stories as *The Invisible Intruder, The Mystery of the 99 Steps,* and *The Clue of the Whistling Bagpipes*. I had dismissed my daughter's new-found fiction addiction, despite being interested in the Hardy Boys books when I was growing up almost 30 years ago. As I finished the tenth Nancy Drew book with Madison, however, I began to notice some commonalities, some consistencies, and, dare I say, some similarities that were reflected in almost every honorable leader that I had interviewed over the preceding two years.

Make no mistake about it, Nancy Drew is not sexy. She'll never be accused of being glamorous. There's no such thing as steamy sex scenes in the Nancy Drew series. As a matter of fact, besides kissing her dad, the famed attorney Mr. Drew, there has yet to be a make out session that includes any characters in Nancy Drew. Murders are extremely rare and Nancy Drew solves her mysteries with her mind and instinct, no guns allowed. Unlike many teen books, music, and movies marketed today, cursing is strictly prohibited. In fact, Nancy Drew never raises her voice. She is, indeed, a courteous young lady. Today's television shows, movies, and books seem to feed off the truly outrageous in a continually escalating manner. But Nancy Drew, and to a lesser extent the Hardy Boys, have been extraordinarily successful even though the literary characters remain what most people would consider to be exceptionally boring. Yet Nancy Drew has staying power. Consider the evidence. Nancy Drew began in the 1930s with the *Secret of the Old Clock* and as book reviewer Meghan Gurdon puts it, "survived the Depression, two world wars, and two waves of feminism." In a media savvy world where sex, glamour, and "pushing the envelope" seem critical to sales, Nancy Drew is still successful.[1] How can this be?

Honorable leaders do not fit the Hollywood model.

It may seem like I'm getting all excited about Nancy Drew. Let me interrupt to regain my manhood. I'm not excited about Nancy Drew *per se*, but I am intrigued because the honorable leaders whom I met and interviewed over the last two years demonstrated some of these same characteristics. Nancy Drew does not fit the Hollywood model. And neither do honorable leaders.

This brings to mind a quote from General George Patton who once said, "If everyone is thinking alike, someone isn't thinking." In reality, those that lead from the high ground don't think like most leaders and deviate dramatically from the widely held script of what a Hollywood leader should be. This should be of no surprise as I mentioned in early chapters, honorable leaders do not pretend to be what they are not. Rather, they tend to *be*.

Dour, lemon-sucking Lieutenant General Thomas "Stonewall" Jackson (West Point, 1846), whose untimely death may have cost Robert E. Lee victory at Gettysburg, was fond of saying, "I have no talent for seeming."

Like Stonewall Jackson, "Old Blue Light" to the troops who revered him, there is nothing outwardly outrageous, headline grabbing, or over-the-top about most honorable leaders. Usually, they are anything but sexy, glamorous, or spotlight-seeking. Yet, they are tremendously effective and, like Nancy Drew, they have incredible staying power. Like Stonewall Jackson, honorable leaders have little "talent for seeming."

Lunch Pail

Frank Beamer, Virginia Tech football coach, ranks among the very best in wins of any Division 1A football program. One of his secrets is his lunch pail mentality to the game of football. In fact, every week during the season a player is given the lunch pail award for the teammate who comes to practice ready to roll up his sleeves and work. This lunch pail award is about getting the job done, about sacrifice, and about getting the hands dirty. It is about doing work that isn't always recognized, which is why Frank Beamer gets the admiration he does. He calls attention to work that often goes unnoticed. Most of Coach Beamer's players who win the lunch pail award are either defensive or special team players—the ones who do not, if ever, win the crowd over with touchdowns. There is little doubt that there is a blue-collar feel about this recognition.

Honorable leaders eat out of the same lunch pail. There was a decidedly blue-collar air among all the honorable leaders that I interviewed. You couldn't help but feel that these people loved the act of leading. They weren't afraid of doing the little things, the things that will never bring glamour. In general, these people never actively sought the limelight and were comfortable without it.

> *Honorable leaders eat from a lunch pail.*

Like Nancy Drew, or baseball immortal Cal Ripken Jr., honorable leaders come to work consistently and are reliable when they work. What I'm saying is, they don't take any plays off. They don't miss a game—remember, they are 24/7. But at work, they tend to be consistently calm and they control their own behaviors. This seemed to be reassuring to those who followed these honorable leaders. Remembering that human beings like to make sense of their environment, when leaders are consistent and not unpredictable, there's a comfort that makes following a leader easier.

Those who lead from the high ground tend to maintain what my navy friends call an "even-keel." Referring to sailors' expertise with ropes ("lines") and knots, mariners also speak of "keeping an even strain." Without an "even strain," a line may snap. Obviously, this is a radical departure from the Hollywood scripted leader in two ways. In Hollywood fiction, the leader only rises during times of crisis and conflict. This is not true on the higher elevations. Here, real leaders lead all the time, not just in crisis, which happens rarely in most organizations. Also, these leaders do not create artificial conflict so they can practice their leadership. This, by no measure, should be confused with the notion that honorable leaders are so consistent that they resist change. In fact, that can't be further from the truth. In every one of the honorable leaders I met, there was a spirit of continual improvement, a deeply held belief that the individual or group had to change for the better. What it does mean, though, is that leaders on the high ground approach change in an even-keeled, comfortable, and calm manner. Assumed in this approach is that if the leader confronts a challenge with arms flailing and excited, others will follow suit. Put plainly, honorable leaders have a knack for seeking control or calm in chaos. To those on the high ground, a strongly held belief is that great leadership is not revealed during times of chaos or crisis. Instead, it is exercised by preventing that crisis or chaos from happening in the first place. In summary, leaders on higher elevations use their leadership and their vision to head off a crisis before it occurs.

Many of these leaders also tended to be better listeners than talkers. The driving force behind this may be the fact that they care less about themselves and more about others. The men and women with whom I talked on the high ground were not the most talkative or the greatest orators of our generation. Rather, they listened first, and when they did talk, they tended to use blunt, but polite and courteous, language. Honorable leaders really are a study in modesty. There is no pretense to impress. They are who they are. They talk that way. They have "no talent for seeming." And they eat out of a lunch pail. While some leaders may need a corner office or a fancy title to feel important, honorable leaders dismiss these gilded trappings of contrived importance.

> Honorable leaders are remarkably humble leaders.

Job Seekers

Honorable leaders seem to possess a thirst for responsibility. From what I've seen in my own military and corporate experience, leaders of all stripes fall into three distinct categories. First are the people who actively avoid responsibility. When the tough jobs come down, they don't raise their hand and they hope they don't get chosen. If they do get chosen, they do whatever they can to escape the job or task. The second category is people who won't raise their hand, but, if chosen, will try hard to accomplish the mission. Finally, there are "responsibility seekers," to use the phrase of Laura Vetter, the former academic adviser to the Kansas State football team and later West Point instructor at the Center for Enhanced Performance. To her, one of the effective ways that West Point develops honorable leaders is by giving young men and women increasing levels of responsibility, while holding them accountable for results.

> *Those who lead from the high ground thrive on responsibility.*

Time and again, this theme emerged during conversations with honorable leaders at West Point, in the military, and within the civilian sector. While it might be a stretch to compare honorable leaders to addicts, it seems that there is, indeed, a craving, an addiction, if you will, to responsibility. Sadly, this is one addiction that is not rampant in society. Look to 2005 Hurricane Katrina relief efforts. The mayor of New Orleans, Ray Nagin, blamed the state and federal governments for poor performance. The governor of Louisiana, Kathleen Blanco, blamed the city and federal governments. Then there is Michael Brown, the former director of the Federal Emergency Management Agency (FEMA), who in Congressional testimony in late September 2005 blamed local and state governments in Louisiana as "dysfunctional."[2] Nothing against any of these people and I'm sure that they're not bad people, but certainly they aren't leading from the high ground when they blame others for their own failures. Part of high-ground, responsibility-seeking behavior is that honorable leaders retain responsibility and accept accountability whether things go well, or, like they did in Louisiana, if things go bad. Good, bad, or indifferent, once higher elevation leaders get responsibility, they're highly unlikely to push it off on somebody else under difficult circumstances. To them, responsibility never stops. Even when Captain Edward Smith released his officers and men as the *Titanic* foundered in April 1912, he still reminded his gallant and doomed crew, "Be British, boys; be British."

Eat Last!

Physiologically, we are hardwired to follow self-preservation tactics and strategies especially in times of danger. The notion of save yourself or "every man for himself" illustrates the genetic drive in most people to put their self-interest above others. This genetic code in our time has mutated into something much more dangerous. In our era of plenty, greed may still be the order of the day. Some CEOs and senior executives who make millions upon millions per year have pursued only selfish interests. Former TYCO CEO, Dennis Kozlowski, spent over a million dollars of TYCO and stockholder money for a party in Sardinia for his wife's birthday.[3] Honorable leaders don't do that.

High elevation leaders open their own lunch pail last, after everyone else has eaten. This duty to eat last can be seen literally in many U. S. Army units in the field where an honorable leader will send all the soldiers through the chow line first to make sure that they are well fed. If there is anything left after all the soldiers have eaten, including the cooks, the honorable leader will sit down for food.

Beware of leaders who eat first. Chances are, you won't see them to your left and right upon the high ground.

The foremost biographer of Robert E. Lee in the Twentieth century was Dr. Douglas Southall Freeman, editor of the Richmond, Virginia, *News Leader* for 34 years. He won the Pulitzer Prize in 1935 for his four-volume biography, *R. E. Lee*, and again in 1958 (5 years after his death) for his seven-volume biography, *George Washington*. He lectured frequently at the Army War College, the Naval War College, and the Armed Forces Staff College. Lecturing at the Naval War College on May 11, 1949, Dr. Freeman declared, "Look after your men. Look after your men ... [T]hat is the sum observation of my travels: Look after your men."[4] Dr. Freeman understood that, on the battlefield or in the boardroom, honorable leaders eat last.

I looked at many cases regarding this point. At West Point, in small business, in non-profits, and in large corporations. Here, maybe among all others, West Point seems to really have a competitive advantage compared to other organizations. Laura Vetter noted, "Firsties [West Point seniors] are taught to think for a unit, rather than thinking for their own self-interest. To focus on the benefit of the unit. It seems that down on Wall Street and in Manhattan the common theme is 'get yours before somebody gets theirs.' Here, self-interest is punished."

Generally, the people you meet on the high ground will be a fairly loyal bunch. And if they are truly honorable, it is likely that their loyalty is constructed in layers. One place I saw this was in the West Point *First Semester Values Education Guide* (2003 edition). Toward the end of this rather extensive and sophisticated training manual, I came upon what West Point calls, "the hierarchy of loyalty." It starts at the lowest level with loyalty to oneself. Then it recognizes loyalty to one's friends. Then to a team. Then to the West Point Corps of Cadets. Next on the hierarchy is loyalty to the Professional Army Ethic. At the top level, West Point expects their leaders to be loyal to the United States Constitution. Realistically, I'm not sure if every level of loyalty could, or should, apply to non-military and civilian organizations. However, when I look over the transcribed interviews, I do notice that almost every honorable leader, military and civilian, progressed substantially beyond the first stage of loyalty, loyalty to oneself. If you want to recognize who these people are, you can find them eating out of their lunch pails, away from the glare of the spotlight, and only after everyone else has been fed.

Kicking and Screaming!

Listen to Colonel Dan Zupan, alum from the 82nd Airborne Division, and one of the more senior officers within West Point's department of English:

> Probably the only time the operations officer and I got a case of the ass with each other was [when] we deployed down to Camp Blanding, Florida. We jumped in there. February. Colder than *hell*. And we had everything wired tight. Except the heater. And we were sitting in this cold-ass tent one night and I thought the ops officer was supposed to bring it. And he thought I was supposed to bring the heater. And the commander, Colonel Baron, said, "Okay, how are we going to fix it?" Real calm. Didn't get angry about it. Never was there any screaming, yelling, or threatening.

One of the characteristics of honorable leaders is that they are, like Colonel Baron, always on an even-keel. They don't scream. Indeed, I found this to be true of all honorable leaders regardless of the setting. But underneath the surface, there is more. The story that Colonel Zupan tells is a vivid example of the patchwork of contradictions that honorable leaders exhibit. The culture of this unit, the elite 82nd Airborne Division, is a decidedly performance-oriented one. Still, this Colonel Baron was able to create a non-threatening, performance-oriented environment. This may not strike you as important, but, from a leadership vantage point, it can make all the difference in the world.

As I talked more with Colonel Zupan, it became clear that a non-threatening, non-screaming culture is important because of its impact on how people deal with mistakes and with the non-linear ascent up the hill. Although honorable leaders create an environment where mistakes are not welcome, errors aren't ruthlessly punished either. Honorable leaders accept that individuals, teams, and organizations are fallible and that it is impossible to create a zero-defect leader or follower. When people know that mistakes are not met with ruthless and overly harsh punishment, they are less inclined to cover them up. Thus, fair

> *Higher elevation leaders don't welcome mistakes, but when they do occur, they ensure that all learn from them.*

tolerance of mistakes never forces people to compromise their honor by hiding mistakes. Also, and maybe more important, mistakes are seen as an opportunity to learn. Clearly, here there was a communications failure between Zupan and the operations officer that resulted in the unit not bringing down the stove. It would've been easy to punish both for the mistake. Instead, this commander, Colonel Baron, saw the absence of a stove as an opportunity to learn and get better.

Habit Forming

Another trait of honorable leaders is that they have good life habits. Most of the honorable leaders I met demonstrated rather superb attention to detail. This phenomenon only became clear to me as I started to investigate why, how, or under what circumstances did leaders, especially at West Point, compromise their honor.

With few exceptions, poor life habits were either centrally or tangentially involved in cases of dishonor. For instance, I learned of several cases where cadets got in trouble for improper documentation. Some of this was intentional, and in other cases, only sloppy carelessness. I had a chance to actually talk to a West Point graduate who was charged with an honor violation for improper documentation. He was not found guilty of purposely trying to deceive. But when I pressed him about it, he said that he had waited to the last minute to work on the term paper that was the focus of the honor hearing. He had references spread out all over his desk and as time was running out, he tried to remember who and where he cited certain authors, but just ran out of time. Consequently, the documentation was incomplete.

> *There is a remarkably strong correlation between good life habits and the capability to lead from the high ground.*

Honorable leaders tend to the details that others might overlook in order to ensure that they are never put in a position to compromise their honor. This attention to detail manifests itself in how honorable leaders carefully read the directions, ask for clarification when they don't fully understand something, or in how they manage their own time.

Courage under Fire

Every leader with whom I had contact possessed courage. Courage to do things that others would not think of doing. Courage not to run away from a challenge. If ever there was a single finding that resulted from this research, it would be the following maxim: It is impossible to have honor without courage. The reverse is not true. You can possess courage without having honor.

This should be of no surprise and there is little more that needs said with only one exception. Chapters 2 through 7 discuss how to build honor and strengthen the honor backbone, which you'll need to carry yourself, and perhaps others on your shoulders, as you ascend to the summit. I came to see an alternative and pioneering application for those chapters. If we put our *Antennae Up and On, Wash Away the Gray*, are *Big About Small Things, Go All In*, have *Good People Covering our Backs*, and can *Imagine That*, then we will not only build our honor, we will also build our courage.

Intelligent Design

While on one of my four visits up to West Point, I learned of a fascinating story. A rising senior told me of the following situation:

> There was a cadet, a firstie [senior] in my company who was smart enough that she was under consideration for a Rhodes, or one of those scholarships.

Well, we had this Pride Bowl event. Basically, our regiment was tasked with providing a certain number of people per company to support this event. She told our admin sergeant that she would be unable to attend the pride bowl. She said she would be unable to attend because she had mandatory church events on Sunday that she has to be at. The admin sergeant waited until Sunday [and] checked the sign-out book. She had signed out on pass. She wasn't at church, but had been with her boyfriend the entire weekend, and that she didn't get back until 1300 hours on Sunday when she initially told him that she had to do something at 0800 hours in the morning on Sunday. She was found for violating our Honor Code.

My grandfather never made it past seventh grade. He was a first-generation American; his parents were Russian immigrants. At an early age, the family was poor and he was sent out to work to earn money for himself and for the family. In 1961, my grandfather started a small family furniture store, which he called Furniture Galleries. Without any real training in geography, history, calculus, or English composition, he opened the doors to sell furniture and some carpet. One of his first customers was a lady who wanted to buy a rather expensive rug, even by 1961 standards. My grandfather told her that it would be $1,000. She then asked if he was sure. He said, "Absolutely." She wanted reassurance that he would not change the price. He told her that his word was his bond and that the price was $1,000. Period. She told him that she'd take it and would be back tomorrow to pack it up. After she left the store, my grandfather noticed that he had quoted her the wrong price. The Oriental rug was $3,000, not $1,000. To make matters worse, he had paid over $2,000 for the rug. His business was only weeks old and he had made a mistake that was going to cost him $1,000. It was a big enough loss for a starting business that he was afraid it would doom Furniture Galleries. Sure enough, the lady returned the next day and she asked my grandfather if he had changed his mind. The older lady was quite certainly an expert or collector of Oriental rugs and she must've known that my grandfather had made a mistake. Still, he held to his word and sold the rug for what he quoted.

In making sense out of these two stories, several important themes emerge. While my grandfather displayed courage and "took the hit" even at a loss to himself, it wasn't what he *had* that distinguished the two, it was what he *didn't* have that is of particular interest. There is something profoundly counterintuitive to what I'm about to say, but that doesn't make it any less true: Intelligence is no guarantee of honor. My grandfather is, indeed, a smart man, but that has nothing to do with his honor. And that isn't what makes him special; it is his honor, not his smarts, that makes him a high-ground leader. During the course of my research, I could detect only a weak correlation between intelligence and honor. Honorable leaders need to erect an antenna, be big about little things, possess an imagination, pick honorable friends, and wash away the gray. While some level of intelligence is required here, you do not have to be a Rhodes Scholar to build honor. The rise of corporate and white-collar crime provides even greater proof that these two variables (intelligence and honor) are not at all or are only very weakly correlated. Now, you might be wondering about the intelligence levels of most of the cadets, officers, faculty, and staff whom I interviewed at West Point, a place that ranks in the top ten of all colleges and universities in Rhodes, Hertz, Marshall, and Truman Scholarships. After several rounds of interviews, I found the relationship between honor and intelligence to be spurious; meaning that we think they are related, but they are not; they just happen to coexist. What this means is that you can't get honor by focusing only on getting smarter.

Closely related to this point is the fact that while honor is not free, it cannot be bought. For many, this should be reassuring. An Ivy League pedigree does not automatically translate into honor. A six-figure income won't earn it either. Rather, building an honor backbone is something that almost anybody, of any race, any gender, any religion, any educational level, and any socioeconomic level can achieve. The lesson here is straightforward, but profound—honor can be earned, but never purchased.

> Honor is learned and practiced, regardless of age, education, or intelligence.

Front-Page News

In the early to mid 1990s, a common practice was that, on Report Day (R-Day), the day civilians would arrive at West Point for their first day of school, a very senior cadet would stand up in the Hollender Center (a huge arena) and say to the crowd, "You now have 60 seconds to say goodbyes to your family and friends. Do so at this time." In 1990, I did that and said goodbye to my parents and brother and boarded a small bus that took me and others from this basketball arena to a place called "Central Area." As I exited the bus, I met my first upperclassmen, a large, well-built man who introduced himself as Cadet Workman. As the first cadet that I came across in my transition from civilian to military, there probably couldn't be any better than Cadet Workman. Without question, he was physically fit, strong, confident, and had a booming voice. I learned later that summer that Cadet Workman, a high school valedictorian, was a Mormon and was granted a 2-year hiatus from West Point to fulfill his Mormon mission. Because of that, this cadet who was two classes ahead of me actually graduated in my class in 1994. Workman went on to become a military police officer and, later, a Drug Enforcement Administration agent.

In October 2002, Timothy G. Workman was found guilty of voluntary manslaughter for the slaying of a man outside a Roanoke, Virginia, nightspot.[5] Although married with children, the altercation and slaying apparently involved a fight over another woman.

Google is a special type of company. Known for its innovation and its minting of millionaires, another defining characteristic of Google is its unique, visible, and, often quoted, corporate mantra, "Don't be evil." One of their notable departures from corporate behavior occurred during the auction of Google shares for its initial public offering (IPO) that was intended to reward small investors rather than the large underwriters and brokerage houses which typically cash in big during public offerings. In a provocative article by the *Wall Street Journal's* Kevin Delaney, we know things did not go according to their mantra. By August 2004, demand for the IPO was below predictions, so Google cut the initial offering price. Some investors, specifically insiders and directors who had large holdings in the business, decided to cut the shares they were going to sell at this reduced price. Those who didn't sell their shares as they initially agreed did quite well since, at the time of Delaney's article, Google shares were up 256 percent. Apparently, Google allowed these insiders and directors to withhold their shares from sale while strong-arming others to make good on their commitment to sell their shares during the IPO. While other large organizations such as Stanford University were allowed to back out of the IPO altogether, small investors such as Stanford Professor David Cheriton were not allowed to reduce the shares they planned to sell during the IPO. Cleverly, Delaney remarked, "Some investors selling shares in the offering were more equal than others."[6]

Electrical engineering is one of the most difficult disciplines to master. At West Point, the words "Electrical Engineering" strike a particularly sensitive chord. EE304, or the core electrical engineering course, became the backdrop for some of West Point's darkest days. Specifically, an EE304 "take-home" examination was passed around the junior class of the corps of cadets in 1976. More than 150 cadets were separated for honor violations in this incident.

General George C. Patton once remarked, "Success is how high you bounce when you hit bottom." Implied in this statement is a sense that it is possible to achieve greatness, to rebound, and to learn from mistakes.

Present in each case above is a setback either at the individual or the organizational level. Some setbacks are severe enough to become failures. I define "failure" as something that is difficult, if not impossible, to overcome. Thirty years in prison for manslaughter may be just such a case. In contrast to failures, setbacks or stumbles on the slope to the high ground don't have to be fatal. Setbacks need not always produce avalanches. When I look over the histories of the truly great honorable leaders, not a single one of them was immune to setbacks. Most admitted that there were times when they strained their honor backbone by overreaching. However, what differentiated honorable leaders and honorable organizations from others was how they responded to such setbacks. This phenomenon is probably best captured by Lieutenant Colonel Blair Tiger's response to a question that I asked, "What are the ways you assess if the ethical development program is working?" His response:

> I think one of the indicators of a successful program is that, today in the army, we still identify the unethical behavior and it becomes front-page news. While yes, it is front-page news, the prison scandal in Iraq, for example, the issue when you put that in perspective of all the things the army is doing, it's still a

small minority of our actions. We were aghast here when a West Point graduate and a peer of mine was the battalion commandeer who had the soldiers who pushed the two Iraqis off the bridge. But I'm glad we're aghast, and I'm glad we identified that as an ethical violation. Because, if we were to overlook that stuff, our system wouldn't work. It's not good press, but it still needs to be front-page stuff to say, "That's wrong." And when it makes even the back page, I think that's a problem that we're not doing as well as we should. Because I think *we* need to be the ones who raise our hands and say, "That's wrong, and we're not going to tolerate it" the most.

Confronting honor setbacks head-on is a trademark among honorable leaders and organizations. Predictably, this is the opposite of what lower elevation leaders do. Overwhelmingly, their *modus operandi* is to cover up and hide their honor setbacks. Of course, covering or concealing honor setbacks strains the honor backbone more, to the point of breaking. Martha Stewart did not serve jail time in 2005 because of insider trading of ImClone stock. She went to jail for lying to investigators about her 2001 sale of Imclone stock.[7] Having the courage to meet a setback head-on instead of sweeping it under the rug separates the average from the great leaders and distinguishes those who speak about honor from those who actually possess it. Laura Vetter speaks strongly to this point, "By bringing it to the fore, by having it brought/made public, it will be addressed. Address it rather than cover it up!"

> *Confront honor lapses head-on; never hide from them or sweep them under the rug.*

So, while West Point clearly suffered a setback during the cheating scandal of 1976, they did not suffer a failure. And while the dismissal of around 150 cadets is clearly not awe-inspiring, the way in which the academy responded was. After the cheating scandal, West Point opened its doors fully and transparently to the Borman Commission headed by former Projects Gemini and Apollo astronaut Frank Borman (West Point, 1950), who took an in-depth look at the entire honor system, which exposed some serious shortcomings. In addition, the army conducted an even broader study called the *West Point Study Group Report*, which looked at all academy programs and policies. Retired General Andrew J. Goodpaster came out of retirement to assume the post of West Point Superintendent to help the academy change. If one is *Big About Small Things*, it is hard to imagine an honor crisis reaching this point. However, if it ever does, hiding, concealing, or lying, will not inspire change; it will only make it worse. The best thing to do then is to own-up, make it front-page news, and begin to change. Given that even small setbacks are part of the journey to the summit, how an individual or organization responds to that setback prepares the slope for future ascents or, possibly, descents. Incidentally, this should explain why the leaders you'll see on the high ground are eating out of their lunch pails while reading the front-page news.

Overreact

Part and parcel of this sensible, low-key, and even-keel approach to leadership is the fact that, even in responding directly and forcefully to a setback, honorable leaders resist overreacting, which for many is the natural tendency.

Consider traveling down a dark road. The driver falls asleep and drifts lazily off the shoulder of the road. Or barreling down a road, a driver hits a patch of wet leaves. Let's consult the Minnesota Department of Transportation to examine their recommendations on driving through conditions such as this, or the snow, or, even navigating black ice. Picture yourself in this situation and ask yourself how you'd react. What we would plan to do to recover and what we actually do may be two different things. I'd wager that not a single driver's manual recommends that a driver should jerk the steering wheel hard to the left or right. For biological and physiological reasons, words in a driver's manual and years of driver's education often disappear as we lose control skidding, sliding, or slipping. Truth be told, most of us do what years of data and counsel tell us not to do—we overreact. The same could be said of individuals, teams, and organizations that feel themselves losing control as they go through a *moment*. The natural reaction is to overreact, to pull the steering wheel hard to the left or right. But overreaction often makes matters worse. Not surprisingly, a common consequence of overreacting is to, indeed, jerk as hard in the opposite direction as possible. A naturally occurring consequence of this tactic is violation of another's space and encroaching on their lane or jumping the median.

Corporate overreaction to crisis could be seen at Citigroup during the first five years of the millennium. Citigroup had its ethical problems and lost its private banking license in Japan for ethical and rules violations.[8] Citigroup also had been penalized for blurring two administrative functions that should be distinct and separate—analyst research and investment banking. To that end, Citigroup has spent billions resolving its underwriting of firms that were clearly corrupt—Enron, WorldCom, Adelphia, and Parmalat. In 2003, Charles O. Prince succeeded Sandy Weill as the CEO of Citigroup. Almost three years after the change in leadership, Citigroup, while not encumbered by the many ethical problems of its recent past, may be less effective as an organization. The reason for this can be traced back to overreaction. Shortly after taking the helm, CEO Prince went about changing Citigroup's ways. As one *Wall Street Journal* reporter put it, "Mr. Prince has set up a host of oversight committees, hired lawyers for top positions, studied reports and polls, and centralized operations and technology." Maybe most damning is that some of Citigroup's top talent, who behaved honorably, even in the previous tumultuous period, chose to jump ship. No doubt that this is among the most difficult of leadership decisions—when and how hard to respond to a setback. Unfortunately, the usual response is overreaction and punishment of the whole for the lapses of the few. This destroys morale and is often inefficient. The 2005 steroids scandal in baseball is a case in point. Most experts agreed that very few ballplayers use steroids. Baseball Commissioner Bud Selig and Donald Fehr of the player's union were unfairly discredited by the media for their effort to find a solution to the problem without overreacting. To Selig and Fehr, the critical question was how to keep the playing field level without subjecting all baseball players to continuous steroid testing. But regular and unscheduled spot testing of all players became policy in November 2005. Overreaction can affect the overall safety and effectiveness of the individual, team, or organization. Honorable leaders seem to be able to deal with this tension.

It was not during my research that I came across an exemplar of how to deal with a setback. It came as I was reading an article in *ESPN, the Magazine*, indulging my passion of sports.[9]

By all accounts, Luis Castillo was an amazing person. In high school, he was an all-state athlete in football and wrestling. Add to that a 3.9 GPA and the fact that he was a card-carrying member of the math and National Honor Society. He enrolled at Northwestern where he played linebacker in the competitive Big Ten football conference. Once a potential first-round draft pick in his junior year, he saw his draft status plummet after a severe injury, a partially torn ulnar collateral ligament in his elbow. This injury, which had a difficult time healing, reduced his lifting power that is closely monitored during the NFL combine. Castillo turned to steroids to improve his lot before draft day. He got caught. Someone knowledgeable in the sports industry offered the following advice, "Do what every other athlete does and play dumb. We can blame it on the testing, you can say you didn't know what was going into your body. Whatever."

> Dealing with an honor lapse does not require overreacting to it or punishing all for the actions of a few.

Castillo's actual response: "I will not do that. I'm not going to lie. I made a horrible mistake and I'm going to be a man about it." In a methodical, straight, and even-keel manner, Castillo wrote a letter explaining what he did, why he did it, why it was a mistake, why it was not in his character, and why he would not do it again. He sent that letter along with all drug tests from Northwestern (all without incident) to every GM in the league. The San Diego Chargers drafted him in the 2005 draft. He now plays on Sunday.

R-e-s-p-e-c-t

Halfway through the writing of this book, I attended a cousin's wedding. As usual, the wedding vows came and went. Cleaning out the car several months after the wedding and right before I began writing this chapter, I came upon the wedding program that was jammed under the kids' car seat with about 300 french fries. I opened it and read it carefully for the first time. The bride and groom had printed their vows in the program:

In the presence of God, our family and friends, I offer you my solemn vow to be your faithful partner in sickness and in health, in good times and in bad, and in joy as well as in sorrow. I promise to love you unconditionally, to support you in your goals, to honor and respect you, to laugh with you and cry with you, and to cherish you for as long as we both shall live.

It may seem that I'm going all *Nancy Drew* on you again. But I'm not. Maybe because I was writing on the topic, my eyes settled on the 53rd and 55th words—"honor" and "respect." I went back to my interviews, manuals, and observation logs to see whether high-ground leaders recognized the correlation between honor and respect. They did.

Finding these wedding vows rang a bell for me. There was something about those leading from the high ground that, until then, I couldn't put my finger on. Missing from my theories on honorable leadership was this notion of respect, a characteristic demonstrated by each and every honorable leader I came across, military or civilian.

The fact that I missed this is hard to understand since honor and respect are quite highly correlated. So much so that the definition of honor cannot exist without the word respect. This book has examined honor as a noun. Something to possess. To hold. To attain. In explaining the relationship between honor and respect, it is necessary to examine honor not as a noun but as a verb. To define a verb, as a former soldier, I am mindful that former president and General of the Army Ulysses S. Grant (West Point, 1843) saw himself as a verb rather than a noun. Racing throat cancer to finish his massive *Memoirs* weeks before his death—a book bankrolled by humorist Mark Twain and designed to rescue Grant's family from bankrupcy—Grant could no longer speak. So he scratched out a longhand note to his doctor, "I think I am a verb instead of a personal pronoun. A verb is anything that signifies to be; to do; or to suffer. I signify all three."[10]

When honor is viewed as a verb rather than a noun, it means, according to the *Merriam-Webster Dictionary*, "the showing of usually merited respect." This makes perfect sense. When we honor the fallen or the dead, we are paying them our respects. When we honor somebody, we are offering respect and esteem to another. Honoring is nothing more than recognizing the internal worth or value of another.

The amazing thing about all of this is that it is difficult, if not impossible, to engage in honor, the verb, if one does not possess honor, the noun. The noun precedes the verb in this case. Demeaning, yelling, screaming, or devaluing another person is an act of dishonor and is less likely to come from a leader who possesses honor, the noun.

Leaders on the high ground mastered taking their honor, the noun, and making it an active-voice verb. The Simon Center for the Professional Military Ethic at West Point has built a RESPECT program on this very notion of honoring and respecting others. West Point believes that if you honor and respect yourself and others, then you are less likely to be culturally and religiously intolerant. Honoring and respecting yourself and others means that a leader is less likely to abuse drugs or alcohol, or engage in destructive personal habits. Since respect and honor are predicated on recognizing the value and worth of others, the idea goes that honorable leaders able to shift honor from a noun to a verb are less likely to commit sexual harassment or racial insensitivity that devalues another human being.

It is difficult to overstate what I observed during my interaction with those who lead from the higher elevations. Simply, they were quite respectful to me and, in their remarks, of others. It was easy to picture these leaders leading not by yelling or screaming, but by harnessing and respecting the diversity of ideas found among their followers. Similarly, it was hard to imagine these people exploiting or using people for their own gain. That, of course, is not respectful, and honorable leaders just don't do that. The main takeaway from all of this is that respecting employees, peers, or a boss, can be accomplished through the pioneering application of one's honor. Another logical extension of this finding is that if you want to get the most out of your sexual harassment, equal opportunity, or diversity training, the place to start may be to invest in honor and character development. The reason is simple. From honor comes respect.

Balance Sheet

A particularly interesting thing occurred as I was finishing a panel interview at West Point. Included in this panel interview were several officers of all ranks and a couple of cadets. I commented to a research assistant shortly after this interview that I've yet to see that quality of human capital gathered in a single place at one time. Among the group was Lieutenant Colonel Brian Mennes, who to many must be West Point's version of action hero, Jean-Claude Van Damme. When I had talked to him, he had recently returned from a tour in Iraq. His answers to my questions were marked with confidence, intelligence, and conviction.

> To honor means to respect.

Throw in there Captain Brian Wortinger, a West Point graduate and recent Darden MBA. Soon to get promoted to major, this young man showed remarkable depth and creativity in all of his answers. If not at West Point, Brian would certainly be making it big on Wall Street—he was that smart. As I was winding down my interview with this brain trust, I noticed that I forgot to ask the Why? question or the Who cares? question. All provided some rather astute answers to the who, what, when, where, and, in particular, the how of developing honor. But when it came to the Why? or Who cares?, there was an awkward moment of silence. Nobody moved. And for the only 30 seconds of the 1.5-hour panel interview, complete silence fell upon the group.

Because the answer to "Who cares about honor, anyway?" was so deeply ingrained in the very bones of these honorable leaders, not one could put it into something as ethereal as mere words, a mere vibration of the breath.

The reason to put into action what you learn in this book or the motive to build personal, team, and organizational honor lies in the answer to the *Why*. In fact, it is impossible to overstate the importance of the *Why*.

Perhaps, the best way to approach the Why? question or to assess the value of honor is through what I call the "balance sheet" approach. A balance sheet is used by individuals especially when applying for a mortgage. Organizations use and report balance sheets all the time. Balance sheets then are a financial snapshot of your personal or organizational financial position at any given time. To get at the net worth, the balance sheet makes it easy. Just examine liabilities and assets for the answer. Hopefully, there will be more assets than liabilities and you'll have a positive net worth.

In regard to honor, it is the liability portion of the balance sheet that shows up again and again. Assumed in this approach to honor is not the question, What value do I get by instilling honor? Instead, the question is inverted to What liability do I incur by *not* having honor? This liability perspective explains the sometimes-cynical public views about honor, ethics, or character. The problem is not in the notion of honor; the problem is much deeper. To use honor not to increase assets but to reduce liabilities drives the cynicism and, ironically, handicaps the individual or organization in the ascent to the top. Using honor only as a tool for risk management is the common belief among leaders in the lower elevations. I'll explain some of the weaknesses behind this single-minded and shortsighted approach, but first I'll explain its existence.

That the perception that the presence of honor and ethics training can reduce liabilities is correct. You may be wondering how this can be. In the early 1990s, the Federal Sentencing Guidelines for Organizations (FSGO) were established to prevent fraud and corruption within organizations. There are two defining characteristics of the FSGO. One, the FSGO's primary mechanism to deter unethical behavior was a system of heavy fines and probation conditions. Two, linking honor to criminal liability, within the FSGO there was room for discretion to reduce penalties if organizations had mechanisms in place to prevent corruption and fraud, such as ethics training.[11]

> *Don't view honor only as a way to reduce liability. Think beyond that.*

There are serious problems with the intent and implementation of the FSGO. The substantive portion of the FSGO is after-the-fact or remedial in nature. The system of fines and penalties goes into effect *after* the corruption has already occurred, been exposed, and prosecuted. For workers who lose their jobs or investors who lose their retirement savings, this after-the-fact or *post hoc* approach to addressing honor lapses is of little solace. Also, the clause stipulating that penalties may be reduced if a firm can show ethical safeguards in place has amounted to nothing more than window dressing. Sure, organizations create honor programs, but the intent is not pure, nor is it progressive. For many institutions of recent infamy, honor-related programs were in place, but were never in use. I'll let you be the judge of whether or not the FSGO has been successful in preventing fraud, corruption, and lapses of honor.

This liability mindset as it relates to honor is the real problem. Liabilities are a drain on a person's or organization's financial health. The more the liabilities, the greater the drain. So, according to the liability model, the only thing that honor and "ethics officers" can do is to lessen the drain. Does that sound like a person or an organization seeking to achieve a competitive advantage? Of course not. It is using honor to reduce liabilities, not to add value. Although honor can reduce liabilities, using honor to do only that is like buying a top of the line computer only to use the calculator function. A microprocessor can do so much more than perform basic math functions. Why not use the computer to its full potential, its full capability. What I'm saying here is that reducing liabilities represents only about 1 percent of what honor can do for an individual, team, or organization. And arguably, it is the least important 1 percent. Those who lead on the high ground know better.

Competitive Advantage

Leaders and organizations that sit on their high-ground perch enjoy so much more than avoiding liability. Reducing liabilities will never translate into a competitive advantage. Honor can do so much more. The best people, teams, and organizations recognize honor truly belongs on the other side of the balance sheet, under "Assets." Evidence suggests that honor may be one of the most potent balance sheet assets.

In the early 1990s, researcher Jay Barney coined what he called the Resource Based View of an organization, commonly known in academic parlance as the RBV.[12] This perspective has gathered support due to its theoretical simplicity. Better than many other theoretical perspectives, it seems to explain why some organizations enjoy a competitive advantage and others do not. Barney contends that assets or resources lead to a competitive advantage. But not just any resource or asset. The asset of greatest worth must be Rare, Valuable, Inimitable, and Non-substitutable, or to use the common acronym—R, V, I, and N. Forms of capital that aren't rare, that add little value, that can be imitated, or that can be easily substituted for, will never lead to a competitive advantage. Consider all the usual assets an organization has at its disposal: technology, financial capital, and buildings, to name a few. Most of these assets can be copied, can be imitated, are not very rare, or can be substituted with a different asset. There may be a ceiling to how much real-value technology, financial capital, or production plants can provide.

How does human capital or honorable human capital satisfy the conditions of V, R, I, or N? Clearly, honorable leaders and honorable organizations have enormous value, are rare, are difficult to imitate, and are not easily substituted for. We have an asset, honorable leadership, which leads to a competitive advantage. But when honor is involved, the advantage is compounded.

When two assets, particularly human in nature, merge, their net value in Barney's RBV model becomes even more difficult to copy or to imitate. Magic can occur when two honorable people meet and interact. The product of such interaction is a special asset that is V, R, I, N to the maximum. It is called *trust*.

Nowhere is this competitive advantage more pronounced than at West Point. Not to say that it doesn't exist elsewhere, but I found that I could almost "touch" or "feel" trust at West Point. For sure, I did witness trusting relationships elsewhere throughout my research program. Maybe due to the amount of time I spent at West Point, I felt it there the most. Notice, I am relying on words like feel or sense. As Jay Barney might predict, trust and the institutional culture that emanates from trust is difficult to sketch, draw, or even describe.

The West Point and United States Army Public Affairs Offices generously granted me permission to conduct my research on the West Point post.[13] That meant I could stay at West Point to interview and observe how they went about growing their leaders. I pushed my luck to see if I could actually live on post, for which I was again given approval.

> *Out of honor comes trust and competitive advantage.*

I had thought about staying at the famed Hotel Thayer, but there were two problems here. First, was the sheer expense. Second, the distance of the Thayer from the cadets, faculty, and staff, would mean that I wouldn't get to observe people in their usual settings. An unexpected solution appeared.

After only three conversations with Lieutenant Colonel Blair Tiger, of which, only two were in person, he turned to me and said, "Stay at our place." I had not even asked; he just offered.

"What? I can't stay at your place for a month. Besides, Blair, I want to bring my family up."

"Bring them along, too! We'll be in Spain during that time, but we want you to have our house during that time."

"Blair, I hardly know you. You don't know me."

"That's Okay. I trust you. Please accept and enjoy."

"Can I pay you?"

"Now you're making me mad. Stop. The answer's No."

When a Ranger-trained army officer tells me he's getting angry, I stop. And we accepted. When the time came to move our family and books and computers up to Blair's house on post, it was the most efficient handoff I had ever experienced. There were no contracts to sign. No deposits to pay. Being recently removed from industry, I forgot that people could do things without contracts and complicated provisions. But there was more.

"Don't worry about locking doors," he said casually.

"What?"

"No, don't worry about it. A lot of times we don't lock our doors. Car doors. House doors. Any type of doors. We may lock the doors, but if we do, it is only to teach our kids the habits that they'll need when they leave West Point."

Imagine a place where you needn't worry about locking the doors. That place exists.

This struck a chord for me as I remembered that I never had a lock for my door as a cadet here. I asked a young man who just finished his plebe year about locking his doors. He thought I was crazy for bringing up the issue. In a tone bordering on dismissive, he made it clear that he never locks his room door. In how many college dormitories could somebody leave their room totally unlocked or unguarded? Let me give you one more example of what a culture of trust looks like.

During the day, I worked out of the West Point library, jotting notes, analyzing the interview data, or reviewing the West Point manuals and training guides on leadership. For about 20 days I worked out of that library. In every case, when it was time for me to eat lunch or interview somebody away from the library, I did the unthinkable. I left my laptop out and on and also left my backup digital voice recorder out in the open. It was a quasi-experiment. I was testing whether honorable theory and teaching correspond to honorable practice. Here, West Point and its honorable culture earned a perfect score. Not once were any of my valuables, including a 5-pound, IBM Thinkpad disturbed.

Sure, from honor comes respect, but from honor also comes trust—the key variable in providing high-ground leaders a competitive advantage. Very quickly, I will elaborate on how trust can improve competitiveness. The real launching point is how trust transforms the communication system between individuals or teams, and within an organization. When people trust each other, they tend to communicate frankly, openly, and honestly. When people trust each other, they are less likely to obscure their communication with political submeanings and undertones. This, in turn, improves both the quality and speed of communication. When people say what they mean without hesitation, ideas can flow quickly and efficiently through an organization. When honest and open communication can spread quickly through these trusting relationships and links, the organization becomes more efficient and effective.

Reflect on the relationships that you've had where trust was and was not involved. When people don't trust each other, be they husband–wife or employee–boss, considerable time is spent verifying and checking. Imagine how much time and energy is saved by taking someone at his or her word without looking over your shoulder? How much simpler and efficient would life be? After my last trip to West Point, I jotted down some figures for the amount of time I saved by not having to pack my laptop or lock my doors over the course of a month. I saved about 4 hours during that time by not having to worry about those things. Imagine how many hours would be saved in an organization of 50 people, of 500 people, if they didn't have to do just those two things. Whether it is a single relationship, a team, or an entire organization, groups are transformed when they no longer have to rely on excessive monitoring and controls to ensure that people do what they say.

Another major factor that leads to a competitive advantage is the waning of self-interest in favor of close collaboration. West Point and the army try their best to produce every army unit in this fashion. It is difficult to do, but, when done, produces tremendous results. Army Rangers, Special Forces, and other famous units, are noted for this type of cohesion. Any organization can achieve this. In fact, while working as a manager within the Target distribution division, I experienced such a feeling of camaraderie. I personally witnessed other managers donating one of their vacation days to a colleague so he could take care of some family matters. When self-interest is tabled in favor of collaboration, coordination, and cohesion, true synergy can occur. Synergy is a phenomenon where two plus two no longer equals four, but equals some multiple of four, like sixteen. Admittedly, it is difficult to reach this state, but it is impossible to get there without honor and trust. Whoever coined that old adage about nice guys (and gals) finishing last never experienced the competitive transformation that results when honor and trust are breathed into a relationship, team, or organization. The challenge that those on the high ground have mastered is the ability to instill this trust asset into the culture of their relationships, their teams, and their organizations. When this is done, you've got an asset, not a liability, and true competitive advantage is yours.

STAND YOUR GROUND

Eleanor Roosevelt once remarked, "No one can make you feel inferior without your consent." This same important principle applies to honor. Once earned, you, and only you, can give it away. Never do that.

Chapters 2 through 7 help build the arsenal to secure the high ground. Once Secured, you must *Stand* that ground. By right, that ground is yours. You earned it and now you own it. And this just isn't any piece of swampland. On the contrary, your ground is quite special because it is the high ground.

When you *Stand Your Ground*, honor becomes the cornerstone of how you lead, communicate, and make decisions. Realize that when you Stand, you are really standing *for* something while simultaneously standing *against* something else. Standing your ground means you stand for strong leadership, honor, respect, fairness, and humility. In kind, when you

Trust transforms.

stand your ground, you stand against doing the easy thing as opposed to the right thing. You stand against injustice, self-interest, and corruption. These are some contradictory views, but the views from the top are never what they were from the bottom. So define yourself. Stand your high ground. And do great things.

Appendix 1

Research Methodology

To answer my research questions, I launched a comprehensive research strategy involving repeated visits to West Point. During a two-year period, I made four visits to the academy with much of that time spent in residence. Specifically, I logged just over 980 hours on the West Point grounds between 2004 and 2005. While there, I conducted in-depth interviews with a diverse sample of volunteers including cadets, staff, and faculty. Using a purposeful sampling technique, I captured an even mix of staff and faculty who were graduates and those who were not. As far as ranks of faculty and staff are concerned, I captured contractual civilians, captains, majors, lieutenant colonels, colonels, and the dean of the academic board, a brigadier general. These staff and faculty served in a variety of positions. In my sample, I had English professors, staff from the Simon Center for the Professional Military Ethic, attorneys, and economics and math professors. All of the Active Duty Army faculty and staff had at least 10 years of service with some approaching 30 years service. Many of the leaders whom I interviewed served and led on battlefields in Afghanistan and Iraq. In general, my sample of West Point faculty and staff was well educated with all possessing some form of advanced graduate degrees. Most earned these degrees from places like Duke, Notre Dame, University of Illinois, Massachusetts Institute of Technology (MIT), and the Rensselaer Polytechnic Institute (RPI). A small portion of those to whom I talked possessed doctorate degrees in their areas of specialty.

My cadet interviews involved all ranks, both genders, and a mix of ethnic and racial backgrounds. All cadets volunteered to be interviewed. None were coerced. In an effort to attain a true picture of their leadership development, I made a concerted effort to interview cadets away from West Point buildings—in non-threatening environments. In certain circumstances, I conducted interviews in social settings like a dinner meal. To allay any fear of reprisal and to encourage honesty, I guaranteed anonymity when requested or needed. For reasons that I address throughout the book, the cadets spoke honestly and courageously regardless of location or context. The ages of the interviewed cadets were between 18 and 23. Accompanying me on three out of the four visits were one of two well credentialed research assistants—a senior doctoral student in Organizational Behavior from Boston College and a senior executive and former employment/labor law attorney. Both provided invaluable help and insight when interpreting the interviews and examining the West Point leadership and honor training documents.

One of my key concerns was the applicability of this data to non-military organizations. To assess the feasibility of transferring such practices, I set out to interview West Point graduates and non-West Point graduates in the private and government sectors. My purpose here was to assess the validity of my findings by asking a simple question—Can you apply the West Point principles uncovered here to you or your own situation?

Here, I conducted a series of field and phone interviews with fifteen West Point alumni who had graduated at least 10 years earlier. In addition, I talked with ten business managers who graduated from an institution other than West Point. Again, to ensure that most of these principles would apply elsewhere, I assembled a diverse sample of working professionals. They included the following:

- A CEO of a privately held food distribution firm, which was the seventh largest privately held firm in South Carolina
- A successful entrepreneur who established a political consulting concern in Ohio
- The CEO and president of a small, successful, retail furniture business in Western Pennsylvania
- A senior quality engineer at a large international conglomerate
- A midlevel manager at a national home builder
- A senior marketing executive at a large, international, retail clothier
- The CEO and president of a privately owned midsized road construction business
- A former VP of operations of a Fortune 500 telecommunications firm.

In addition to the interviews, I carefully examined over 500 pages of West Point documents that detail and describe the West Point Leadership System. These include the *Cadet Leadership Development System, West Point Honor System and Procedures, Values Education Guide, Hip Pocket Values Education Guide, Cadet Basic Training Values Education Guide, Cadet Field*

Training Values Education Guide, New Cadet Character Development Workbook, and *West Point White Paper for the Cadet Honor Code and Honor System.* I also reviewed the program for the 2003 and 2004 National Conference on Ethics in America that West Point annually hosts. I also had the luxury of talking to the president of the Western Pennsylvania West Point Parent's club, John Gould, who, at the time, had both his son and daughter enrolled at West Point. At times, I also personally observed leadership and ethics-based training.

Appendix 2

West Point Fact Sheet[1]

Mission: "To educate, train, and inspire the Corps of Cadets so that each graduate is a commissioned leader of character committed to the values of Duty, Honor, Country and prepared for a career of professional excellence and service to the Nation as an officer in the United States Army."

Location: The Academy is located approximately 50 miles north of New York City on the west bank of the Hudson River in Orange County, New York. West Point is America's oldest, continuously occupied military installation, first garrisoned on January 20, 1778. The U.S. Military Academy, located on just over 16,000 acres, was established by an Act of Congress on March 16, 1802.

Cadets: The 4,000 members of the Corps of Cadets represent every state in the U.S. and several foreign countries. About 1200 new cadets enter the Academy on Reception Day each year (about July 1st). Approximately 16 percent of the Corps of Cadets are women.

Admission: To be considered for admission to West Point, a candidate must be at least 17 but not yet 23 years of age on July 1st of the year of admission. Candidates must be qualified academically, medically, and physically and must receive a nomination from an approved source, such as a member of Congress. For the Class of s2009, 8,422 men started an application file and 1,062 were accepted. 2,351 women started an admissions file with 189 offered entry to West Point.

Academic: In addition to a core curriculum, balanced in the arts and sciences, and a required five-course engineering sequence, similar to a minor, cadets may select from one of a possible 42 majors. Classes are small, usually less than 18, and the faculty to student ratio is among the lowest in the nation—1 instructor for every 8 students.

- 70 percent of the Class of 2009 graduated in the top fifth of their high school class.
- About 70 percent of the Class of 2009 scored at least 600 on the verbal portion of the SATs.
- About 80 percent of the Class of 2009 scored at least 600 on the math portion of the SATs.
- The average SAT score of an incoming cadet is just shy of 1300.
- Of the 1,251 incoming cadets of the Class of 2009...
  - 102 were high school valedictorians
  - 37 were high school salutatorians
  - 215 received National Merit Scholarship recognition
  - 766 belonged to the National Honor Society
- Rhodes Scholar ranking (as of November 1, 2005)
  Harvard–287
  Yale–190
  Princeton–164
  West Point–84 (Fourth)
  Stanford–70
- Hertz Scholar ranking (as of November 1, 2005)
  MIT–99
  Stanford–62
  Princeton–40
  West Point–37 (Fourth)
  Harvard–36
- Marshall Scholar ranking (as of November 1, 2005)
  Harvard–97
  Princeton–54
  Stanford–46
  Yale–42
  MIT–35
  Brown–30
  West Point–27 (Seventh)
- Truman Scholar ranking (as of November 1, 2005)
  Harvard–30
  Yale–27

West Point–24 (Third)
Duke–24
Stanford–23

Physical: Physical education and athletic participation occur throughout the four years, with 25 varsity sports and numerous intramural and club sports available. All cadets are required to compete in a competitive sport every year. These activities can range from intramural athletics to Division 1A intercollegiate activities. Also, every cadet must take physical education classes. Mandatory classes include boxing for men, self-defense for women, survival swimming, and gymnastics. In addition, all cadets must repeatedly complete a cadet physical fitness test consisting of push-ups, sit-ups, and a 2-mile run during their four years. Cadets must also successfully pass an indoor obstacle course as part of their physical development. Of the 1,251 incoming cadets of the Class of 2009

- 1,138 played varsity sports in high school
- 1,094 earned a varsity letter in their high school sport
- 781 were the captain of the high school sports team

Military/Leadership: Cadets are placed in a variety of leadership environments during and outside the 10 month academic year. All cadets participate in cadet basic training their first summer and cadet field training during their second summer. During their third and fourth summers, cadets can either serve as training cadre for the incoming class or can participate with active duty military units worldwide. All cadets experience at least 47 contact hours of moral-ethical enrichment over the course of their four years. Of the 1,251 incoming cadets of the Class of 2009

- 228 were Boys/Girls State delegates
- 252 were their high school's class president
- 500 were scouting participants
- 175 earned either the Eagle Scout (men) or Gold Award (women)

TIMELINE

1802—Thomas Jefferson signs legislation establishing the United States Military Academy at West Point.
1803—Three cadets graduate.
1808—The "Father of the Military Academy," Sylvanus Thayer, graduates. Thayer would assume the duties of Superintendent barely a decade later.
1810—There was no class of 1810 due to Congressional funding shortfalls.
1815—"Cadet gray" becomes West Point's official color.

1823—George Sears Greene graduates second in his class. Greene would later become the founder and President of the American Society of Civil Engineers.

1826—On December 24, 1826 West Point cadets launch an egg-nog riot where cadets ran down officers at sword point and launched missiles through windows. As a result, several cadets were court-martialed.

1828—Jefferson Davis, the President of the Confederacy, graduates toward the bottom half of his West Point class.

1845—Thomas Jonathan "Stonewall" Jackson began his final year at West Point. Through persistence and hard work that is recognized to this day, Jackson continually rose in class rank over his four years. He graduated 17 out of 59.

1852—Robert E. Lee named West Point Superintendent.

1865—West Point's mark on the Civil War is undeniable. Many historians recognize 60 major battles. Amazingly, 55 of those battles had West Pointers commanding on *both* the Union and Confederates sides.

1877—Henry O. Flipper overcomes tremendous obstacles to become West Point's first African-American graduate.

1886—John J. Pershing graduates. Pershing would later become the commander of the American Expeditionary Force in World War I. He is the only officer to attain the rank of General of the Armies.

1887—Dining hall is named Grant Hall after Ulysses S. Grant.

1890—First Army-Navy football game is played on November 29, 1890. Navy wins 24–0.

1903—Cadet Douglas MacArthur graduates. To this day, MacArthur is recognized as achieving among the highest academic and military records of all graduates of the Long Gray Line.

1909—George S. Patton Jr. graduates. Unlike MacArthur, Patton has difficulty and is held back a year for his poor showing in math.

1910—The Cadet Chapel is completed. The chapel organ is the largest in the Western Hemisphere.

1915—Dwight D. Eisenhower and Omar N. Bradley graduate.

1919—General Douglas MacArthur appointed Superintendent. MacArthur is largely credited for formalizing and encouraging the development of the West Point Honor System. MacArthur also establishes a formal intramural program.

1936—William Westmoreland graduates as First Captain (the highest ranking cadet) in his class of 1936. Westmoreland would later serve as Superintendent from 1960 to 1963 and then later as commander of U.S. forces in Vietnam.

1943—West Point graduates a class in three, as opposed to four years to get more officers in World War II.

1944/

1945—Army wins back to back national championships in football with the help of Glenn Davis and "Doc"Blanchard (in 1946 Army finishes second in the polls behind Notre Dame).

1958—Cadet Pete Dawkins wins the Heisman Trophy.

1962—General of the Army Douglas MacArthur gives one of the most famous speeches, "Duty, Honor, Country," ever recorded at West Point while receiving West Point's highest honor—the Sylvanus Thayer award.

1966—Rhodes scholar and future Supreme Allied Commander in Europe, Wes Clark, graduates.

1968—Mrs. Elizabeth Lewis becomes West Point's first female faculty member.

1969—Two West Point graduates, Major Mike Collins and Colonel Edwin "Buzz" Aldrin go to the moon.

1970—Major General Samuel Koster is relieved as Superintendent over the My Lai massacre.

1979—Vincent K. Brooks is appointed West Point First Captain—the first African-American to achieve the highest cadet rank.

1980—First West Point class to graduate women.

1989—Kristin M. Baker is the first woman to command the Corps of Cadets.

1998—West Point cadet, Alison Jones, wins the Soldier's medal, for her heroic efforts during peacetime to rescue the injured during the bombing of the American embassy in Narobi.

Notes

INTRODUCTION

1. "Baby formula? The locked case at the front of the store," *New York Times,* 5 June 2005, 33. Also, excerpts can be found at http://www.msnbc.msn.com/id/8088953 "Powdered baby formula goes behind the counter" June 4, 2005.

CHAPTER 1

1. Joanne B. Ciulla, "The importance of leadership in shaping business values," *Long Range Planning* 32, no. 2 (April 1999): 166–173.

2. Stephen E. Ambrose, To learn more about West Point and its rich history please refer to *Duty, Honor, Country: A History of West Point* (Baltimore: Johns Hopkins University Press, 1999) and Theodore J. Crackel, *West Point: A Bicentennial History* (Lawrence: University Press of Kansas, 2003).

3. Susanne Craig and John Hechinger, "A Wall Street affair: This bachelor party gets lots of attention," *Wall Street Journal,* 18 July 2005, A1, A8. Susanne Craig and John Hechinger, "Fishing for Fidelity business, One firm employed lavish bait," *Wall Street Journal,* 11 August 2005, A1, A7.

4. Joy Thompson, "Ex-Morgan CEO to sell $40 million in stock," *USA Today,* 15 July 2005, B1.

5. Stephen Venables, *To the Top: The Story of Mount Everest* (Massachusetts: Candlewick Publishers, 2003).

6. Frank Borman and Robert J. Serling, For a remarkable story of an officer, astronaut, and senior executive refer to *Countdown: An Autobiography* (Silver Arrow Publishers, 1988).

CHAPTER 2

1. Keith L. Alexander, "1.86 Flights: too good to last," *The Washington Post,* 19 April 2005, E01.

2. US Airways online blog, http://blogs.flyertalk.com//blogs/viewwing/archives/2005/04/usairways_to_ho.html, accessed October 20, 2005.

3. Boeing CEO Philip Condit resigned in December 2003 after it was found that Boeing hired a top Defense Department procurement official, Darleen Druyun (and her daughter), at about the same time it was bidding on an $18 billion contract for aerial refueling tankers. Roughly a year after this incident, Harry C. Stonecipher, the CEO replacing Condit, stepped down after admitting to an extramarital affair with another executive. Byron Acohido and Jayne O'Donnell, "Extramarital affair topples Boeing CEO," *USA Today*, 8 March 2005, B1. Lynn Lunsford, Andy Pasztor, and Joann S. Lublin, "Boeing CEO forced to resign over his affair with employees," *Wall Street Journal*, 8 March 2005, A1, A8. Andy Pasztor and Rebecca Christie, "Boeing Ex-Officer pleads guilty in hiring case," *Wall Street Journal*, 16 November 2004, A2.

4. From 1996 through 2002, the United States Air Force Academy confronted sexual harassment and, in 2005, cases of religious intolerance. Kellie Lunney, "Defense investigates sexual assaults," *Government Executive* 35, no. 9 (July 2003): 16. David Van Biema, "Whose God is their co-pilot," *Time* 165, no. 26 (27 June 2005): 61–63.

CHAPTER 3

1. Sue Shellenbarger, "How and why we lie at the office: From pilfered pens to padded accounts," *Wall Street Journal*, 24 March 2005, B1. Can also be found at CareerJournal.com, www.careerjournal.com/columnists/workfamily/20050325 workfamily.html.

2. Mark Whitehouse, "Closing the deal: As banks bid for city bond work, 'Pay to Play' tradition endures," *Wall Street Journal*, 25 March 2005, A1, A4.

3. For more information refer to the following articles by Ian McDonald: "Moving the market, Marsh's results are hurt by loss of commissions," *Wall Street Journal*, 3 August 2005, C3 and "Moving the market, Former Marsh brokers, executives are indicted in bid rigging case," 16 September 2005, C3.

4. Ellen Byron, "Spitzer charges former CEO of Federated with perjury," *Wall Street Journal*, 5 January 2005, B1, B2.

5. Michelle O'Donnell, "DeNiro's maid is accused of theft," *The New York Times*, 22 July 2005, B-6.

6. Gary Klein, *Sources of Power: How People Make Decisions* (Cambridge: The MIT Press, 1999) 1–14.

7. Kara Scannell, "Executives on trial: Quattrone's lawyers in appeal argue for dismissal of charges," *Wall Street Journal*, 28 January 2005, C4.

8. Monica Langley and Theo Francis, "How investigations of AIG let to retirement of longtime CEO," *Wall Street Journal*, 15 March 2005, A1, A16.

9. Kevin J. Delaney, "In 'click fraud,' web outfits have a costly problem," *Wall Street Journal*, 6 April 2005, A1, A6.

CHAPTER 4

1. Barbara Hagenbaugh and Matt Krantz, "New Accounting Rules Raise Price Of Audits: Cost Of Compliance On Companies," *USA Today*, 13 April 2005, 1B.

2. Barbara Hagenbaugh and Matt Krantz, "New Accounting Rules Raise Price Of Audits: Cost Of Compliance On Companies," *USA Today*, 13 April 2005, 1B.

3. Jeffrey B. Arthur, "Effects Of Human Resource Systems On Manufacturing Performance And Turnover," *Academy of Management Journal* 37, no. 3 (June 1994): 670–688.

4. Shawn Young and Deborah Solomon, "Qwest engaged in fraud, SEC says; Agency alleges misdeeds were led by top officials; Firm to pay $250 million," *Wall Street Journal*, 22 October 2004, A3.

5. Julie Schmit, "Drugmaker to pay $300M to defer case," *USA Today*, 16 June 2005, B1. Stephanie Saul, "Fraud case field against ex-officers of Bristol-Myers," *The New York Times*, 16 June 2005, C1.

CHAPTER 5

1. Chris Moneymaker, For the entire Chirs Moneymaker story please refer to his autobiography, *Moneymaker: How an Amateur Poker Player Turned $40 into $2.5 million at the World Series of Poker* (New York: HarperEntertainment, 2005).

2. Wayne Barrett, Please refer to the following controversial biography of Guiliani *Rudy! An Investigative Biography Of Rudolph Guiliani* (New York: Basic Books, 2001).

3. James Bandler and Joann S. Lublin, "Inside MassMutual scandal, An angry wife sparked probes," *Wall Street Journal*, 19 August 2005, A1, A14. James Bandler and Joann S. Lublin, "MassMutual board fired CEO on finding 'willful malfeasance.'" *Wall Street Journal*, 10 June 2005, A1, A5.

4. Andre Laurent, "The cultural diversity of Western conceptions of management," *International Studies of Management and Organizations* 13, no. 1–2 (1983): 75–96.

5. Aaron Lucchetti and Kara Scannell, "How day traders turned squawk-box chatter into profits," *Wall Street Journal*, 23 August 2005, A1, A8.

6. Eric Rice, Gary Slyman, and Albert Pierce, *Ethics for the Junior Officer*, 2nd Ed. eds. Eric Rice, Gary Slyman, and Albert Pierce. (Annapolis: Naval Institute Press, 2001), 11, 147.

CHAPTER 6

1. Len Marrella, *In Search of Ethics: Conversations with Men and Women of Character*, (New York: DC Press, 2001) 35. For the complete transcript of the speech preceded by an excellent discussion please refer to pages 27–54.

2. Jeff Opdyke, Evan Perez, and Ann Carrns, "Behind New Orleans's flood: Three unseen waves of water," *Wall Street Journal*, 7 September 20005, A1, A6.

3. For more information access http://www.sleepfoundation.org/hottopics/index. php?secid=10&id=249.

4. Cris Prystay, "Five are charged in case involving CAO Singapore," *Wall Street Journal*, 10 June 2005, A6, A7.

5. Sylvia Pagan Westphal, "Boston Scientific to pay $74 million to settle stent case," *The Wall Street Journal*, 27 June 2005, B4.

6. John M. Higgins, "Sins of the father and a son," *Broadcasting and Cable* 134, no. 28 (12 July 2004): 12–13.

7. Shawn Young and Peter Grant, "More pinstripes to get prison stripes," *Wall Street Journal*, 20 June 2005, C1, C2.

8. Daren Briscoe, "The new face of witness protection," *Newsweek* 145, no. 18 (2 May 2005): 56. Tom Jackman and Jerry Markon, "Northern Virginia Gang Members Indicted," *The Washington Post*, 16 December 2004, B01.

9. Peter Maas, The life events of Frank Serpico are well chronicled in *Serpico The Cop Who Defied the System* (New York: Viking Adult, 1973). For more on the concept of lamplighting, refer to Frank Serpico's official website at: www.frankserpico.com.

10. George. C. Herring, *The Pentagon Papers*, Abridged Ed. (New York: McGraw Hill, 1993). Daniel Ellsberg, *Secrets: A Memoir of Vietnam and the Pentagon Papers*, (New York: Viking Press, 2002).

11. Richard Lacayo, and Amanda Ripley, "Persons of the Year: Sherron Watkins of Enron, Coleen Rowley of the FBI, Cynthia Cooper of WorldCom," *Time* 160, no. 27/1 (30 December 2002-6 January 2003): 24–31.

CHAPTER 7

1. Chuck Salter, "Protect this house," *Fast Company*, August 2005, 70–76. Robert J. Terry and Rachel Sams, "Under Armour moves for IPO," *Baltimore Business Journal*, 26 April 2005.

2. Ken Sakamoto, "The flop that flabbergasted," *Honolulu Star Bulletin*, 13 February 1999, Sports Saturday Section.

3. Ruth Kanfer, "Motivation theory and industrial organizational psychology," in *Handbook of Industrial & Organizational Psychology*, 2nd Ed., eds. M. D. Dunnette and L.M. Hough (Palo Alto: Consulting Psychologist Press, 1990), 75–169.

4. Albert Bandura, To appreciate social cognitive and learning theories refer to *Social Foundations of Thought and Action: A Social Cognitive Theory*, 1st Ed., (New York: Prentice Hall, 1985) and Albert Bandura, *Social Learning Theory*, (Englewood Cliffs, NJ: Prentice Hall, 1977).

5. James Randi, For more on Nostradamus please refer to *The Mask of Nostradamus: The Prophecies of the World's Most Famous Seer* (New York: Prometheus Books, 1993).

6. Charles Forelle, "Seeking restitution, government targets TYCO duo's riches; A long list of assets includes homes, $17 million yacht and 350 head of cattle," *Wall Street Journal*, 30 June 2005, A1. Yochi J. Dreazen, "Volcker Panel Rips U.N.'s oversight, pushes for change," *Wall Street Journal*, 7 September 2005, A3. Yochi J. Dreazen, "Volcker probe is unable to resolve questions regarding U.N. officials," *Wall Street Journal*, 8 September 2005, A2.

CHAPTER 8

1. Megan Cox Gurdon, "The world according to Nancy Drew," *Wall Street Journal*, 16 September 2005, W8. The entire history of *Nancy Drew* can be found in Melanie Rehak, *Girl Sleuth: Nancy Drew and the Women Who Created Her* (New York: Harcourt, 2005).

2. Andrea Stone, "Ex-FEMA chief blames locals," *USA Today*, 28 September 2005, A1.

3. Stanley Bing, "A meeting in Sardinia," *Fortune* 148, no. 11 (24 November 2003): 256.

4. Stuart W. Smith, "Douglas Southall Freeman on Leadership," ed. Stuart W. Smith, (Shippensburg, PA: White Mane Publishing, 1993), 175.

5. "Roanoke jury finds man guilty of manslaughter," *Roanoke Times*, 26 October 2002. "Defendant takes stand in murder trial," *Roanoke Times*, 25 October 2002.

6. Kevin Delaney, "Google IPO revisited: Insiders got choice other sellers didn't," *Wall Street Journal*, 16 September 2005, A1.

7. Alan Abelson, "The Trendsetter," *Barron's* 85, no. 10 (7 March 2005): 5–7.

8. Monica Langley, "Behind Citigroup departures: A culture shift by CEO Prince," *Wall Street Journal*, 24 August 2005, A1, A8.

9. Seth Wickersham, "Full disclosure," *ESPN: The Magazine*, 26 September 2005, 50–56.

10. Ulysses S. Grant, *Memoirs and Selected Letters* (New York: The Library of America, 1990), 1120.

11. Dawn-Marie Driscoll and W. Michael Hoffman, "Gaining the ethical edge: Procedures for delivering values-driven management," *Long Range Planning* 32, no. 2 (1999): 179–189.

12. Jay, B. Barney, "Firm resources and sustained competitive advantage," *Journal of Management* 17, no. 1 (1991): 99–120.

13. It is important to note that West Point never censored the book. In addition, West Point never asked or received any compensation or royalties from this book.

APPENDIX

1. Fact sheet derived from information provided by the West Point Public Affairs Office and the official website of the United States Military Academy, usma.edu. Also, please refer to Theodore J. Crackel, *West Point: A Bicentennial History* (Lawrence: University Press of Kansas, 2003) for a complete and comprehensive listing of key dates and a fuller appreciation of West Point's long and storied history.

Index

About the Author

EVAN H. OFFSTEIN is Assistant Professor in the Department of Management at Frostburg State University. A graduate of the United States Military Academy at West Point and a former military intelligence officer, he also served as an Instructor in the Department of Management, Virginia Poytechnic Institute and State University. He is also certified as a Senior Professional in Human Resources (SPHR). He has published articles on leadership, management, and corporate competitiveness in such journals as *Business Communication Quarterly*, the *Journal of Managerial Psychology*, the *Journal of Engineering and Technology Management* and *Human Resource Management Review*. To learn more about Evan or honorable leadership, visit www.honorableleaders.com or email Evan directly at eoffstein@frostburg.edu